Learning from
Classmates

LISA EICKHOLDT

Learning from
Classmates

Using Students' Writing
as Mentor Texts

FOREWORD BY STEPHANIE HARVEY

HEINEMANN
Portsmouth, NH

Heinemann

361 Hanover Street

Portsmouth, NH 03801–3912

www.heinemann.com

Offices and agents throughout the world

Cataloging-in-Publication Data is on file at the Library of Congress.
ISBN: 978-0-325-05091-1

Editor: Holly Kim Price
Development editor: Alan Huisman
Production: Hilary Goff
Cover and interior designs: Monica Ann Crigler
Typesetter: Kim Arney
Manufacturing: Steve Bernier

Printed in the United States of America on acid-free paper
19 18 17 16 15 PPC 1 2 3 4 5

Dedication

■ ■ ■ ■ ■ ■ ■ ■ ■ ■ ■ ■ ■ ■ ■ ■ ■ ■ ■ ■

For all that I am and ever hope to be,
I owe to my angel mother.

—*Abraham Lincoln*

This book is dedicated to the memory of Jean Snyder:
my mentor, most cherished friend, and mother.

Contents

Foreword by Stephanie Harvey

We were cruising up I-285 from the Atlanta airport to Gwinnett County when Lisa Eickholdt first shared her idea for the book you hold in your hands. Whenever I come to Gwinnett, Lisa volunteers to chauffeur me to and from the airport which is one of the highpoints of my Georgia visits. Standstill Atlanta rush hour traffic actually becomes a welcome reprieve as Lisa and I gush all things literacy. "What are you reading?" "Who did you see at IRA?" "Any new lessons?" "Who is your most intriguing student this year?" These kinds of questions fill the car and time evaporates.

Over the course of multiple visits to Gwinnett, I urged Lisa to write something of her own. She was an extraordinary teacher, coach, reader, and writer herself with much to share. I knew she could write about a vast array of literacy topics, so taking Don Graves words to heart, I encouraged her to write about what she knew best and cared most about.

"Writing!" she said in a heartbeat. "Writing is what I am truly passionate about."

"Great, go for it," I said.

"So how do I get started?" she queried. And I quoted Don Murray whose wise advice nudged me to start writing twenty or so years ago. First off, "Put your butt in the chair" and know this—according to Murray, "the only real difference between writers and non-writers is that writers write!"

So Lisa began to explore, research, and write. And just as kids need to narrow their topics to a manageable arena, so did Lisa. She reviewed what was out there and quickly bumped into seriously stiff competition from a host of sagacious writers and writing specialists: Don Murray, Donald Graves, Lucy Calkins, Katie Wood Ray, and Ralph Fletcher to name a few. It seemed that they and many others had pretty much covered the writing PD book publishing world. If Lisa wanted to get published, she needed to fill a void.

After much thought and research, Lisa landed on the topic she cared most about. On yet another airport sojourn, she shared that she really wanted to write a book about how to use kids' writing to mentor other kids. She was committed to showing teachers how much kids can learn from each other. I was blown away by the merit of this idea, but I was realistic. In this standards-based, one-size-fits-all, test-crazed world, would anyone consider publishing such a book?

Enter Heinemann under their "Dedicated to Teachers" banner. They loved the fresh idea and gave Lisa the reins. We are so lucky they did! Lisa's book is magical. What we see happening with kids who really pay attention to other kids' writing is truly inspiring. While no one would argue that Cynthia Rylant is an extraordinary writer, her writing prowess may seem out of reach for many kids. For some elementary age kids, using adult, fully-developed writing as a model for their own writing can only lead to envy and, ultimately, frustration. When we use student writing as mentor texts, many kids believe that quality writing is within their reach and that they can do that too!

This book is chock-full of useful information for developing strong writers. A well-organized arrangement of chapters on immersion, conferring, assessment, and lessons keeps the book engaging and accessible. The conferring chapter features scripts of conferences Lisa has with young writers which give us a clear window into the kids' thinking as well as Lisa's. The lesson chapter is both practical and powerful. Lisa shares small details such as how to best display mentor texts, as well as big ideas and a range of lesson demonstrations that she uses to teach writing. In her lessons,

Lisa sometimes shows the mentor text and shares the strategy that the writer used and has the kids talk about it. Other times, she shows several drafts of the mentor texts, so kids can see how the writing evolved during the writing process. Sometimes she engages in an inquiry approach and has kids notice what they see and wonder about in the mentor text and then discuss what they learned. "Working backward" is an especially effective practice, where Lisa shows the final draft of a child's mentor text and has kids talk about what they think the writer's plan was. Once they have discussed this, the writer shares his or her actual plan.

Ultimately this book is about the power of mentorship. I am proud to have been a mentor to Lisa Eickholdt. But as our friendship flourished, we learned more and more from each other. The roles of mentor and mentee merged. We taught and learned from each other. We mentored each other. That is what this book is finally about: collaborative learning. When we value kids' writing enough to use it to teach other kids, all kids grow into stronger writers. All kids mentor each other. And we teachers learn as much by paying close attention and listening to kids as they learn from us. We mentor them; they mentor us. Thanks, Lisa, for writing this important book. I needed it, teachers need it, and the field needs it.

Happy Reading!

—Stephanie Harvey

Acknowledgments

This is a book about mentoring, so it only makes sense to begin by thanking all the people who have mentored me throughout this journey. This is my first time being published, and I've learned that it takes a lot of people to create a book.

I will be forever indebted to Stephanie Harvey for her help throughout this process. As busy as she is hopping all over the globe, Stephanie still took the time to read my initial proposal. Then, she encouraged me to submit it to a publisher. Later, upon hearing I got a book contract, Steph offered to write the foreword for me. If it weren't for Steph's initial enthusiasm for the idea and her continued cheerleading along the way, I would never have started or continued pursuing what often seemed like an unobtainable goal. Thank you for being both a mentor and friend, Steph.

I am also grateful to Harvey "Smokey" Daniels, who willingly skipped a conference luncheon to help me edit my proposal. What a difference his suggestions made to my writing. I can't thank him enough for his time and help editing and submitting my proposal.

It is with deep appreciation that I say "thanks" to my amazing editor, Holly Kim Price. Holly read my proposal the way I hope all teachers will read their student's writing—through the lens of possibility. She searched for and found, hidden in a very rough draft, a small kernel of something worthwhile. As I worked my way from proposal to manuscript to final copy, Holly supported me. Every time we conferred, she found a way to see through my ramblings to the point I was trying to make. Like all great writing teachers, she never took over the writing, but instead helped me make the book more my own. There are not enough words to thank her for everything that she has done for me.

The book production team at Heinemann, headed up by Hilary Goff, has always made me feel special. When I received a greeting card signed by the whole team with my contract (thanks, Sarah!), I knew this was going to be a special experience. Thanks go out to many people. Alan Huisman, who helped make my writing clear and concise. Monica Ann Crigler, creative genius, who made me cry not once, but twice, because she designed a book which was far more beautiful than anything I could ever have imagined. Thank you to Hilary Goff and Pamela Hunt who put the finishing touches on and made it shine.

This book wouldn't have been possible without the teachers and students at Puckett's Mill Elementary School. The students' writing fills this book and shows the rest of the world what is possible when kids are provided with great instruction by teachers who care deeply. In addition to the incredible teachers and students, my administrative team has always supported me. Thanks go out to Suzanne Pierce, Lesley Pendleton, and Stephanie Stewart—the greatest group of assistant principals ever assembled. Finally, of course, to the great Michelle Farmer, the most fantastic principal a girl could ever hope for. I will always consider working for Michelle and company one of the highlights of my career. It is rare to work so hard, yet have so much fun.

It takes a lot of time to write a book. Time that could be spent in other ways. I am grateful that I was blessed with such an independent and social child. I appreciate how my son, Jack, played with his friends every day after school for hours. His time outside throwing footballs, shooting basketballs, and hitting baseballs allowed me to write. The time we spent apart also helped me appreciate the time we spent together each night talking and, best of all, reading.

Emerson wrote, "Our chief want in life is somebody who will make us do what we can." My husband Keith has always been that person for me. He believes in me more than I believe in myself. Few people have someone who tells them every day that they are smart and talented. When this happens, you start to believe it (no matter if it's true or not), and begin to think you can do something really tough, like get a book published. For this and a million other things, I thank him.

Introduction

The Power of Using Student Writing as a Mentor Text

Education is all a matter of building bridges.

—*Ralph Ellison*

Much of what we know how to do in life we have learned from mentors. Cambourne (1988) demonstrated long ago that children learn how to talk (and can learn how to read) by imitating their parents. In an essay regarding the way humans learn, Smith (1998) asserts that we learn from the company we keep. Learning how to talk, how to walk, how to ride a bike—all these important life skills are taught by mentors. It makes sense to bring this idea into the classroom.

Using children's literature as a mentor text is common practice in writing workshops. Teachers embrace the idea of learning from mentors and fill their classrooms with beautifully written children's literature by such authors as Cynthia Rylant, Patricia MacLachlan, and Vera B. Williams. Nothing is more important to teaching writing than exposing students to beautiful literature. If we want students to *write* beautiful work, they must first *read* beautiful work. Katie Ray (2006) suggests that teachers expose students to a genre before ever asking them to pick up a pen. She calls this part of the prewriting process *immersion*.

Teachers also use mentor texts in writing lessons. Lynne Dorfman and Rose Capelli, coauthors of *Mentor Text: Teaching Writing Through Children's Literature* (2007), share ideas on how to use children's literature to teach just about every conceivable writing technique, from writing a compelling lead to creating a satisfying ending. Mentor texts are extremely important to our teaching.

MY JOURNEY TOWARD USING STUDENT WRITING AS A MENTOR TEXT

In a speech to a group of teachers about conferring with student writers, Anderson (2009) asserted that it's crucial to have an idea of the kind of writing you hope students will do in a unit of study so that you can teach toward those goals:

> It's all fine and good to have Cynthia Rylant in your mind, but she's in a different universe! She's a fine, fine writer, but to look at a third-grade piece and think how do I get from this piece to Cynthia Rylant? Some kids will get there, but it's such a big leap that it's helpful to look at what looks strong on a third-grade level or a sixth-grade level. That helps you think of more reasonable steps to take to guide a kid towards being a stronger writer.

I agree; Cynthia Rylant is a fine writer, and some kids will reach her level, but many won't. When I compare most of my students' writing with the children's literature I use in my classrooms, I see a large chasm between the two. What we all want as teachers is to help more children become better writers. Using student writing as a mentor text can help us achieve this goal.

A few years ago, when I was working as a literacy coach in a local elementary school, a fourth-grade teacher requested my help implementing a writing workshop in her classroom. We decided to launch our workshop with a study of personal narrative writing. After spending some time reading, gathering, and planning, the students were finally ready to draft. One of the first conferences I had was with Rebecca, who decided to write about her first roller-coaster ride at Six Flags because she had previously been too scared to get on one. However, her writing didn't match her intention; the piece was all about the trip to Six Flags. A typical "bed-to-bed" story (Anderson 2005), it began when she woke up that morning and ended with her going home and going to bed. If she wanted this story to be about overcoming a fear, Rebecca needed to focus and angle her story to convey that theme. After helping her plan a new draft that matched her intentions, I left her to write. The next day, Rebecca showed me her revised draft (see Figure Intro.1).

Rebecca accomplished something important in this piece—she made her writing match her intentions—and it offered a unique teaching opportunity. I had spent the last few lessons using children's literature and my own writing to model how writers focus their writing but with limited success. Perhaps my students needed to see what this concept looked like in writing that matched their level of development. If I used "Goliath" as a mentor text, the other students might finally understand what I was trying to teach them. And that's exactly what happened! I watched in amazement as student after student began to change their writing in response to Rebecca's. Their positive reaction led me to search for more student writing to use as mentor texts. The more I looked, the more I found. Adding this new kind of mentor text to my teaching has had a profound effect on my students.

Figure Intro.1 Rebecca, Fourth Grade, "Goliath"

Why Does Using Student Writing as a Mentor Text Work?

Smith (1994) asserts that three key aspects need to be in place for learning to occur: demonstration, sensitivity, and engagement. Demonstration occurs when an adult or a more capable peer models for students. Sensitivity is the feeling that we can accomplish the task at hand. Engagement describes the productive interaction of the learner with the demonstration. Scaffolding, a term coined by psychologist Lev Vygotsky (1978), refers to the support students receive as they learn. According to Vygotsky students have two levels of intelligence. The first level, measured by traditional IQ tests, is what they already know. The second level is what they can learn to do within their zone of proximal development (ZPD)—the distance between what a child can do independently and what he or she can accomplish with the assistance of a more knowledgeable other. The distance between these two levels of development is bridged through scaffolding. When we use student writing as a mentor text, we are using all three of Smith's learning concepts, along with Vygostky's notion of scaffolding.

Demonstration

In Rebecca's fourth-grade class, I initially scaffolded her learning when I demonstrated a new writing technique for her during our conference. Later, after she revised her piece, Rebecca went from mentee to mentor when she demonstrated how to apply a particular strategy in writing for the other students.

Sensitivity

For learners to be willing to take on a task, they must feel they stand a reasonable chance of succeeding. Students who had not been affected by the texts I had shared in previous minilessons changed in response to Rebecca's work. Seeing her writing raised their level of sensitivity (self-efficacy). They had a more developmentally appropriate model, something they could aspire to more easily. In addition, they knew the writer. Schunk and Hanson (1985) found that students responded with more self-efficacy and achievement after they watched a video of a peer modeling than after watching a video of a teacher modeling. Rebecca was a peer—someone the students played with, ate with, and rode the bus with; this similarity built self-confidence.

Engagement

When we lift students' self-belief, we automatically lift their engagement with a task (Johnston 2004; Rist 2000). Others have noticed the positive effect great student writing has on students. Anderson (2000) writes, "This is one source I wish I had taken more advantage of when I was a classroom teacher. Without fail, when I showed a student's piece in a minilesson, the interest level in the class rose exponentially" (131). This increased interest may have to do with the context in which we share our students' writing. In a workshop, we try to convey to students that we value their work in big and small ways, from having students share their writing from the class author's chair to publishing and celebrating student writing beyond the classroom. Featuring a student's work in the lesson—teaching with a student's writing—takes this idea to another level. When we use student writing along with children's literature and our own writing in lessons, we are inviting students to join what Smith (1998) refers to as the "literacy club" (11). Smith believes we learn from the clubs we are included (or excluded) from: "We know who we are from the clubs, both formal and informal which we associate ourselves; from the company we keep" (11). We are also inviting them to join the teacher club. When we weave between these types of mentor texts in our lessons, we are placing students' writing alongside other writers' (children's authors) and adults' (their teacher) whom they admire or aspire to be like.

Additional Benefits of Using Student Writing as a Mentor Text

"Can I take my writing home and finish it this weekend?" Matthew asked as he grabbed his notebook and headed out the door of my classroom.

"Sure, that would be great!"

After he left, I stop to relish this moment. His request is a small miracle. Matthew is in fifth grade and struggles with writing. Because he struggles, he comes to my morning class of reluctant writers to get some encouragement and help. This class is filled with kids that would rather do just about anything in the world than write. So why would a kid who hates to write ask whether he could do more of it, on the weekend no less? I don't think it's coincidental that Matthew volunteered to do extra writing at home on the very day I used his piece as a mentor text in my lesson. Perhaps for the first time in his life, Matthew felt like a "real" writer, and this feeling changed his attitude about writing—a change I've grown accustomed to. Time and time again, I've watched reluctant and unenthusiastic writers become more eager and willing writers after their writing was used as a model for other students.

Research has shown what most of us who teach writing already knew: Students' attitudes toward writing affect their ability to write (Knudson 1995). The reasons for this correlation are obvious. If you want to be good at something, you must practice it. It's also human nature to avoid things we dislike. If we hate to do something, writing say, we avoid it and get little practice at it. Because we avoid it, our skills continue to decline, and we get worse as those around us who keep practicing get better. We fall further and further behind.

The positive change in students' attitude is the most important reason for using student writing as a mentor text. It's the reason I wrote this book. I have spent my career—intervention teacher, Title One teacher, Reading Recovery teacher, Early Intervention teacher, and many things in between—working with struggling readers and writers, kids who hate to write. One of the most important things I've learned is that it's imperative to let every child know we believe in him or her so the child feels valued. In *Choice Words*, Johnston (1994) discusses the power of our words on kids. What we say to children helps them create positive or negative identities. The simple act of calling students writers or poets or researchers helps them envision themselves in these roles. When we use our students' writing as mentor texts, we are helping them identify themselves as someone who writes.

We are also communicating another powerful unspoken message: "I think you are a *good* writer!" Asking a student to share what he or she has written so others may learn from it is the highest praise. The power of praising students' writing cannot be disregarded. Genuine praise from us can "lift the hearts, as well as the pens, of the writers that sit in our classrooms" (Daiker 1989, 112). Once students see themselves in the role of a mentor, they begin to act accordingly. Writing is one of the most personal acts students do in school. Whether intentionally or unintentionally, writers reveal themselves to the reader. "All writing is autobiographical" (Murray 2009). When we let students know we value their writing, we let them know we value them as a person too, something that reaches well beyond the classroom.

Everybody has something worthy to offer. Too often gifted students are the ones who receive acclaim in our classrooms. When choosing writing to use as a mentor text, we must consciously choose to use writing from all students, not only a select few. We need to send the message that we believe everyone, not just certain students, can be a great writer. In order to ensure we include all students in the mentoring process, we need to search for the good in each and every piece of writing we read—a line, a sentence, a few choice words—no matter how small. Bomer (2010) challenges teachers to support all children by posing the following question:

> And what if we were able to champion even the most spindly pieces of writing by digging in and envisioning what is there, assigning the same generous amounts of time and respect we give to the most difficult of published literature? (8)

Let's face it: The children's literature we use in our classrooms is flawless. It has been revised and edited many times. And few question the importance of exposing our students to the best writing we can find. However, the student writing we share in our writing workshops, especially if we use students' ongoing drafts (and we should), will most certainly include spelling and grammatical errors. We should use it anyway. Using work in progress lets students know that we value what they have to say, the unspoken message being that we value them too. If students know we believe in them, that the content of their writing matters, more kids will take a risk and try some new things, even if they don't know how to spell all the words or punctuate all the sentences correctly.

Look again at Rebecca's piece in Figure Intro.1. Like most drafts, it isn't perfectly neat, perfectly spelled, or perfectly punctuated. Yet it is filled with many great qualities, like focus and elaboration. Sometimes we get sidetracked by poor conventions and miss the beauty in our students' work. We become what Probst (quoted in Bomer 2010) calls a "hunter of errors" (18). Our challenge is to look beyond sloppy handwriting, misspelled words, and poor grammar and find all the good in our students' writing. Once we begin to overlook some of the surface errors, we can find what Bomer (2010) aptly calls the "hidden gems" in each student's work.

Recently, I called Rebecca to ask her permission to use "Goliath" in this book. She clearly remembered sharing this piece with the class. After all these years, I could still hear the pride in her voice when we discussed it. Her mother also recalled our work together; she still mentions the story to her daughter's middle school language arts teachers. What seemed simply a wise teaching decision—to make one student a mentor for the others, to use her writing as a bridge for the other students to cross—was something much more important.

BUILDING THE BRIDGE

I was recently in a first-grade classroom that was working on a personal narrative unit. One of my first lessons was on elaboration. In this lesson, I decided to use Jack's writing as a mentor text, pointing out how he elaborated by describing what his character was thinking and feeling. Jack is a struggling writer so one of the purposes of using his piece as a model was to boost his confidence. Highlighting Jack's writing paid off later when I noticed that he was taking a risk with his latest piece. A few minutes into the independent work portion of the workshop, I paused to confer with Christina. I talked to her for a few minutes about her story. As we talked, I decided Christina could benefit from learning Jack's elaboration strategy. Therefore, I decided to use Jack's piece as a mentor text in my conference. The teaching portion of my conference sounded something like this:

> **Me:** You mentioned that you wanted to work on adding more to your piece. Can I help you with that today?
>
> **Christina:** Sure.
>
> **Me:** Great! In our lesson a few minutes ago, we looked at Jack's piece and saw how he elaborated by telling what his characters were thinking and feeling. Let's take another look at his piece and see how he did that. (I pull out a copy of his story and we reread it, paying close attention to how he used this elaboration strategy.) Now it's your turn. Let's read through your piece and see how you can use these elaboration techniques, just like Jack did.
>
> **Christina:** I know where I can do this! Right here on this first page. (She quickly begins to write.)

Jack's story helped Christina instantly understand this elaboration technique, something she wasn't able to see as easily in the polished children's literature we'd read and referred to in previous lessons. Later, in a conference with Joey, I noticed how he elaborated on his piece with purpose and intention. Keeping my group's needs in mind, I made a quick note to use his writing as a mentor text in an upcoming lesson. In fact, with notes from all my writers, I was ready to plan tomorrow's lesson, which would focus on elaborating with purpose and intention.

Using Jack's writing as a mentor text boosted Jack's self-esteem and helped him become more of a risk taker; but using his writing as a mentor text also helped other students become better writers. Conferring with a lens toward finding other mentor texts helped me develop the next few lessons in our writing workshop. It required a few small steps: I immersed the writers in mentor texts, including student writing as mentor texts; I selected Jack's piece during conferences the previous week because I knew from my assessments that some of his classmates could benefit from his elaboration technique; and as I conferred, I set myself up for a highly targeted lesson with Joey's piece. All of this occurred as part of my regular writing workshop, and required only a slight adjustment in how I look at students' writing.

Figure Intro.2 sets out the distinct steps you can take to incorporate student writing into your teaching. Each chapter in this book offers explicit instructions on how to use student writing as a mentor text. I'll show you how to read your students' work with the selection of mentor texts in mind. My notes on conferring and assessment will reveal how I matched writing I'd selected from among my students to other writers' needs. And, finally, you'll get an in-depth look at how to put it all together with planning notes and lesson transcripts. Using your students' writing as a mentor text not only lifts the level of their writing, it lifts their spirits. Perhaps most important, it will affect you as a teacher. If you got into teaching to inspire students (and who didn't?), using your students' writing as mentor texts will help you do just that. Now, go forth and inspire!

Figure Intro.2 Steps to Using Student Writing as a Mentor Text

Immersion

Immerse students in an upcoming genre by reading lots of great writing to them. Choose writing that is filled with the qualities of writing you value so that you may return to this writing again and again throughout the unit.

Assessment

Assess students' writing throughout a unit of study, looking for common needs. Set writing goals and target these concepts in upcoming lessons.

Lessons

Use student writing as mentor texts to help you teach key writing strategies and techniques in your lessons.

Conferences

As you confer with individual students during the unit, keep in mind the writing goals you have set. Search for student writing to use as mentor texts in upcoming lessons.

Immersion

Using the Lens of Possibility to Choose Student Writing

Here's the secret of writing: there is no secret.

—*Ralph Fletcher*

When planning an upcoming unit of study, one of the things to keep in mind is the writing process. Though writing is a unique undertaking, researchers have identified stages or steps that most writers go through. These stages are fluid and overlap, but most agree they include some version of the following: rehearsal/prewriting, drafting, revising, editing, publishing, and celebrating (Calkins 1994; Graves 1983). Therefore, a unit of study should include lessons that help students work through the writing process, as well as lessons on how to make their writing more interesting or lessons on craft.

For many years, the first step, rehearsal (sometimes called prewriting), primarily consisted of helping students generate ideas and plan their upcoming writing. Recently, writing experts have highlighted the importance of reading throughout the process, in particular during the prewriting stage. Katie Ray (2006) believes that before writers put pen to paper they must have a vision for what their writing might look like at the end: "Before revision, vision" (35). To help students with this "prevision," to give them an idea of what they are working toward, many writing experts suggest spending three to five days immersing students in a genre at the start of every unit of study (Bomer 2010; Caine 2008; Ray 2006). As we read through these texts we might also make note of features which are unique to that kind of writing. For example, at the start of a unit on all-about books, I might examine several mentor texts and make an anchor chart with my students that highlights the key features or big ideas of the genre.

What we notice about informational books:

- They have photographs or very accurate pictures.
- Most have a table of contents.
- Most have a glossary.
- Some have an index.
- Most have print that is darker (bold font).

- Most books are divided into chapters.
- There is writing under the pictures (captions) and around the pictures (labels).

Later, I can return to these same texts and focus in on one part of the writer's craft in a lesson—highlighting how a writer concludes an informational text, for example.

CHOOSING STUDENT WRITING TO USE FOR IMMERSION AND BEYOND

In addition to using children's literature during immersion, I also use student writing. To help me choose student writing for immersion, I use a form based on the work of Katie Ray.

Notice, Name, and Note

Date:

Title of Piece/Author:

Notice: What do I notice about this piece? What part(s) do I really like?

Name: Where have I seen this technique before? What is it called (literary term)? What might we (the students and I) call this?

Note: Why does this make the writing better (more interesting, easier to envision, clearer)? How did the writer probably go about using this technique?

Notice

Obviously, choosing mentor texts starts with reading. After students have enjoyed the text as a reader, I can then go back and ask them to read it like a writer (Ray 1999). Reading like a writer begins by simply paying attention. I pause and notice the things I find beautiful in a text: the parts that move me to laughter or tears, the sections that make me want to keep reading; this is craft. As soon as I notice the craft, my mind immediately shifts to writing teacher mode: Because I know that though, "writing is individual, it is not unique" (Ray 1999). What I notice in one text is something I've probably seen in another. More important, this technique has a name.

Name

Two anonymous quotations come to mind here. The first is, "Recognition leads to replication." The second is, "You can't claim it if you can't name it." The point in both is that in order for something to be repeatable, it must first be given a name. This idea is important to all teaching but it is of particular importance to the teaching of writing: When students know the name for a specific writing technique, it is much easier for them to emulate it. Because naming is so critical to writing, I let students invent their own labels for some of the literary techniques we are studying. For example, students often decide to call a simile *making a comparison*—a better description of what a writer is actually doing. Because the name is more specific, students remember it better and are more likely to use it in their own writing. Whether students invent the name or I provide it, naming is crucial to learning.

Note

After noticing and naming the craft in a piece, I consider why a particular strategy is significant. What makes this writing technique effective? How does it make the text better? Considering how a particular writing technique improved a piece helps me explain to the students why they should use it. I also consider how the writer implemented the technique. Identifying the steps in a writer's process helps me explain them to my students.

Examples of Noticing, Naming, and Noting Student Writing

The following student samples help kids immerse themselves in their respective genre. These touchstone texts (Angelillo 2003) also offer many opportunities for making teaching points in future lessons. I'll suggest a few, and you'll find many more.

Informational Writing Samples

There are many different types of writing which fall under the umbrella of informational text, including all-about books, how-to texts, and narrative nonfiction. Though it is tempting to have students begin by writing research pieces in an informational unit, I have found it helpful to ask students to begin by writing about topics they know well first, and later move into some research pieces.

"Snakes Fantastic!" (Figure 1.1)

This is an "all-about" book. Ashley wrote about snakes because she had a pet snake and knew a great deal about them. Though she did some additional research, choosing a topic she was familiar with enabled her to focus on the writing. Writing is easier when students write about topics they know well.

Figure 1.1 Ashley, Second Grade, "Snakes Fantastic!"

Snakes Fantastic!

The Cobras baby

Den

by Ashley

Introduction

Dear reader, The reason I chosed these topic is becase, When I was about 7 years old I went to a zoo and found a sign that said (baby snakes loose in the zoo! Be carful!) And when we came in I came face to face with one. And I picked it up and it did not bit me! It was wierd becase snakes usaley bite. I asked my mom and dad if I could keep it and they said if you spend all the money for it so I did and I named him scales. Thats why I picked this topic.

Love, Ashley. J

What are Snakes

snakes are a part of, a group called **reptiles**. Some Reptiles have scales and some can swm. Some snakes are **venomies** (Posonies). Some snakes have rattes and some can clime trees. Pythons do not have fangs, they sqeeze their prey. Some snakes rap their tailes around their prey. Snakes are cold-blooded. Snakes Hibernate in the winter. Some snakes have more then 1,000 bones in their body. Snakes shed their skin about 30 times a year. Snakes body is always the tempacher of the air.

2

Figure 1.1 Continued

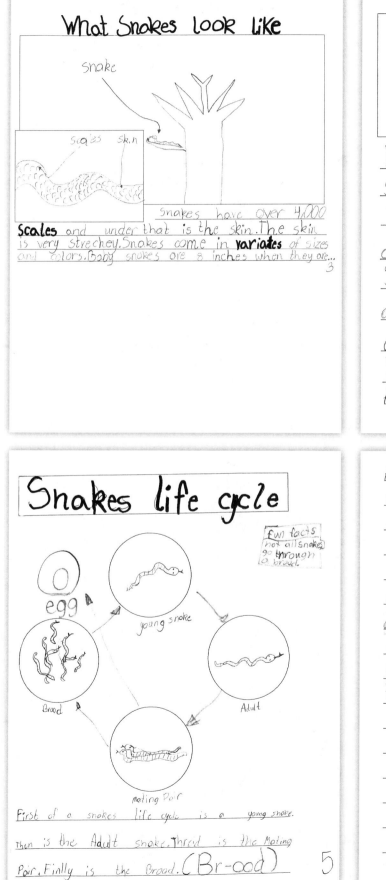

What Snakes look like

snake

scales   skin

snakes have over 4,000 **Scales** and under that is the skin. The skin is very strechey. Snakes come in **variaties** of sizes and colors. Baby snakes are 8 inches when they are...

3

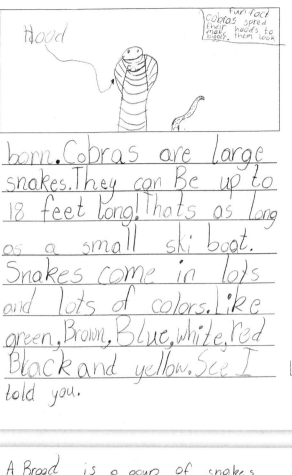

Hood

fun fact Cobras spred their hoods to make them look bigger.

born. Cobras are large snakes. They can Be up to 18 feet long! Thats as long as a small ski boat. Snakes come in lots and lots of colors. Like green, Brown, Blue, white, red Black and yellow. See I told you.

4

Snakes life cycle

egg

fun facts not all snakes go **through** a brood.

young snake

Brood

Adult

mating Pair

First of a snakes life cycle is a young snake. Then is the Adult snake. Thred is the Mating Pair. Finlly is the Brood. (Br-ood)

5

A Brood is a goup of snakes hunting, becase some times it is hard to hunt so they goup up and whatever they find they eat it and Share. A mating pair are two snake that live toogeather and have babies. When baby snakes are born they all ready now how to hunt so off they go.

6

Figure 1.1 Continued

Parts of a Snake

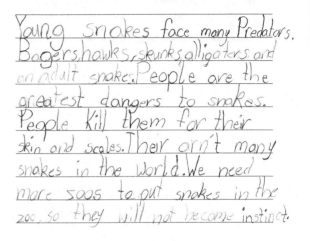

Some snakes have rattles and some don't.
Some snakes have fangs some times the
fangs can be venomis.

Dangers to Snakes

Young snakes face many Predators. Bogers, hawks, skunks, alligaters and an adult snake. People are the greatest dangers to snakes. People kill them for their skin and scales. Their arn't many snakes in the world. We need more soos to put snakes in the zoo, so they will not become instinct.

8

Recards

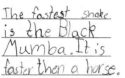

The fastest snake is the Black Mumba. It is faster then a horse.

The heaviest snake is the Green Anaconda. It is as heavey as a 50 men stacked on top of eachother.

The smallest snake is the Lesser Antillean (Lesser -A-talleyon) It is as small as a worm.

Some snakes have two heads.

9

Glossary

Posanise \ venomis

Posanise and venomis are the same thing we are apost to call it venomis, but we call it posanise.

reptiles

reptiles are a group of animals that either have scales or lethorey skin.

Scales

scales are snakes clothes to them they feel bumpy and cover their skin.

Varites

Varites mean alot.

10

Figure 1.1 Continued

Dig deep to find facts about snake.

Notice, Name, and Note

Title of Piece/Author: "Snakes Fantastic!" by Ashley

Notice:
• Bolded words defined in a glossary
• Parenthetical definitions
• Words defined within the body of the text

Name:
• Defining domain-specific vocabulary

Note: A main reason informational text is more difficult to understand is the domain-specific vocabulary. Nonfiction writers must find ways to define key vocabulary within their text. A common method is to highlight the words throughout the text and then define them in a glossary. Alternatively, writers can put the definitions in parentheses after the words or define them within the body of the text. Ashley uses all three methods in "Snakes Fantastic!" She bolds various vocabulary words and then defines them in a glossary. On page two, she defines *venomous* by putting *poisonous* in parentheses after it. And in the section on a snake's life cycle, she defines key vocabulary words within the body of the text; after introducing the word *mating*, for example, she explains what it means in the next sentence: "A mating pair are two snakes that live together and have babies."

"How to Make a Fruit Smoothie" (Figure 1.2)

One of my favorite ways to introduce informational writing is with "how-to" pieces. Primary students can create step-by-step directions for simple tasks such as making a peanut-butter-and-jelly sandwich (or a smoothie in first grader Loan's case). In the upper grades, I often ask students to write essays on how to do the things they know best or consider themselves to be an expert on (see the example in Figure 1.3, by Logan).

Figure 1.2 Loan, First Grade, "How to Make a Fruit Smoothie"

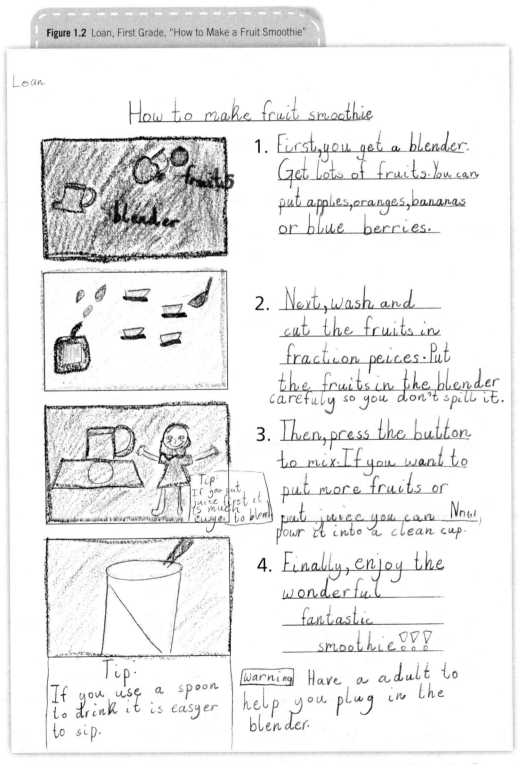

Loan

How to make fruit smoothie

1. First, you get a blender. Get lots of fruits. You can put apples, oranges, bananas or blue berries.

2. Next, wash and cut the fruits in fraction peices. Put the fruits in the blender carefuly so you don't spill it.

3. Then, press the button to mix. If you want to put more fruits or put juice you can. Now, pour it into a clean cup.

Tip: If you put juice first it is much easyer to blend.

4. Finally, enjoy the wonderful fantastic smoothie.

Tip: If you use a spoon to drink it is easyer to sip.

Warning Have a adult to help you plug in the blender.

Notice, Name, and Note

Title of Piece/Author: "How to Make a Fruit Smoothie," by Loan

Notice:
• Extra details that help readers work their way through the step-by-step process

Name:
• Tips and warnings

Note: Tips and warnings give the reader extra information. Tips usually provide ideas that make the task (or parts of it) easier to complete. Warnings include details that help ensure the safety of the reader.

"How to Be a Good Reader" (Figure 1.3)

I introduce the essay with how-to writing I call *expert pieces*. This type of writing helps upper-grade students understand the basic parts of this genre (thesis statement, main ideas, supporting details, and elaboration). The following example, one of my all-time favorites (I'm a literacy teacher, after all) is just one section of a complete essay.

Notice, Name, and Note

Title of Piece/Author: "How to Be a Good Reader," by Logan

Notice:
• The writer uses details to elaborate on each idea.

Name:
• Tell and show

Note: The most impressive thing about this piece is the elaboration. If the secret to a great story is to show, not tell, the secret to a great informational piece is to tell *and* show (Calkins and Gillette 2006). Logan writes, "You need to know that questions are a sign of a good reader [tell]. It is not a bad sign [show]. And then you can write the question on a sticky and put it in the book [show]. A good reader will have a book full of stickies [show]." In the next two paragraphs he does the same kind of telling and showing. Elaboration is the secret to writing well in any genre, and this piece is a great nonnarrative example.

Figure 1.3 Logan, Fourth Grade, "How to Be a Good Reader"

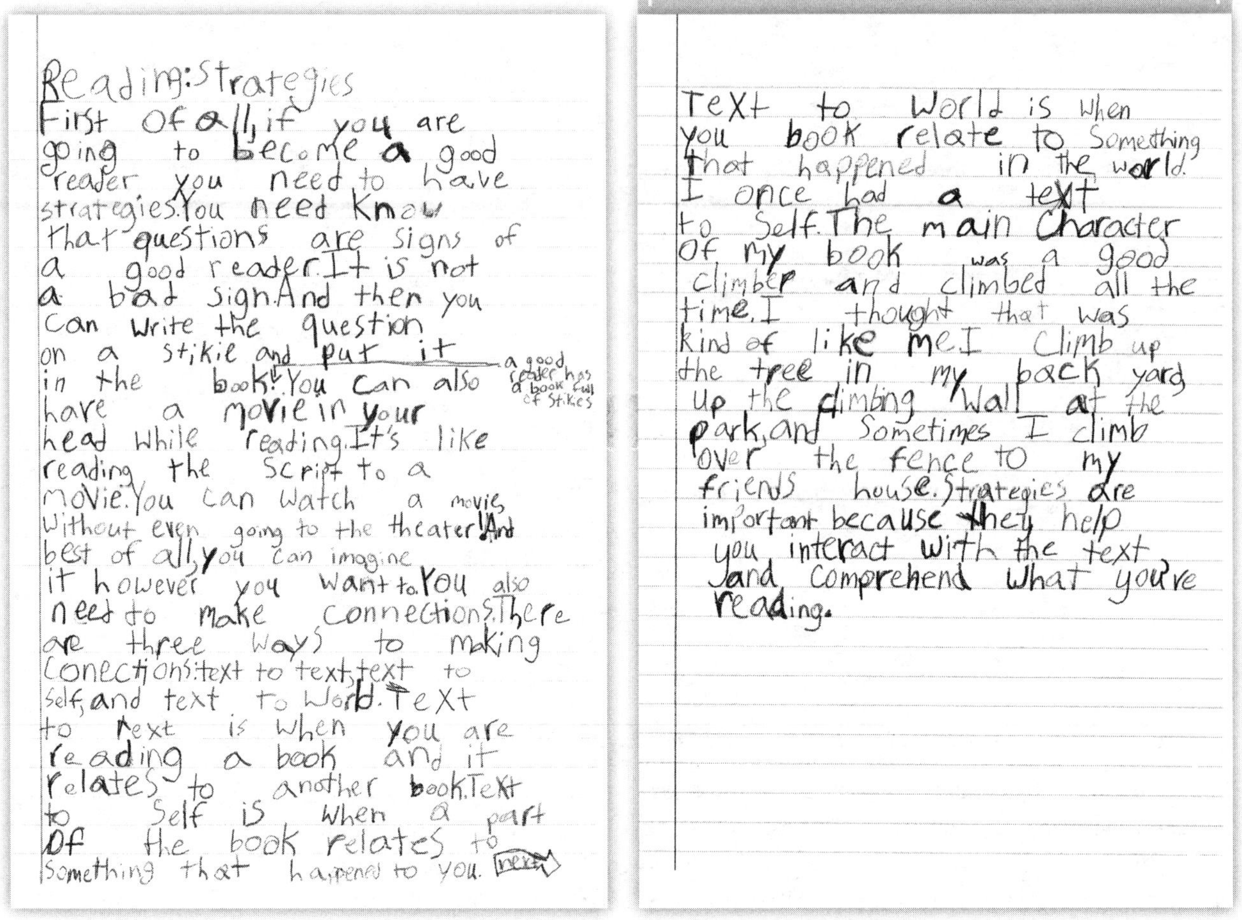

Reading:Strategies
First of all,if you are
going to become a good
reader you need to have
strategies.You need know
that questions are signs of
a good reader.It is not
a bad sign.And then you
can write the question
on a stikie and put it
in the book!You can also   *a good reader has a book full of stikies*
have a movie in your
head while reading.It's like
reading the script to a
movie.You can watch a movie
without even going to the theater.And
best of all,you can imagine
it however you want to.You also
need to make connections.There
are three ways to making
conections:text to text,text to
self,and text to World.Text
to text is when you are
reading a book and it
relates to another book.Text
to self is when a part
of the book relates to
Something that happened to you. *(over)*

Text to World is when
you book relate to Something
that happened in the world.
I once had a text
to Self.The main character
of my book was a good
climber and climbed all the
time.I thought that was
kind of like me.I climb up
the tree in my back yard
up the climbing wall at the
park,and Sometimes I climb
over the fence to my
friends house.Strategies are
important because they help
you interact with the text
and comprehend what you've
reading.

Narrative Writing Samples

A narrative is a story that has a beginning, middle, and end. The story can be a personal narrative where the writer recounts a true story from his or her life, or some sort of fictional narrative (realistic fiction, historical fiction, fantasy, etc.). Though students want to write fictional narratives (and we should include some studies on these), fiction narratives include challenges (inventing characters, setting, a problem and solution) which makes the writing more difficult. This is something you will want to keep in mind when planning this type of study.

"The Great Alpaca Ranch" (Figure 1.4)

I found this story when I was collecting entries for a local student-writing contest. Although second grader Lauren's piece didn't win, it is a beautifully written narrative.

Figure 1.4 Lauren, Second Grade, "The Great Alpaca Ranch"

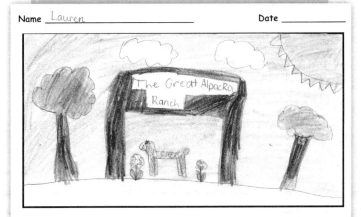

Name Lauren   Date _____

The Great Alpacka Ranch

My family was on an alpacka Ranch. I was was walking along the path way to the big canals where the babies run and have a lot of fun. I heard the crunching of the gravel as I walked. I was walking quickly for a reason. I could not wait to feed the alpackas. I brought a few bright red apples (that were extra sweet) along to feed them. I walked with my head up and happily smiled

to my favorite one named Nely and thought about how to feed her. I broke a shiny slice of apple in half. Snap! I broke it again. Snap! Juice splated on me. Then I carefuly reached through the fence and ran my hand with the small, shiny, and juicy slice of apple under the soft white mouth and waited. Pits Pat! Pits Pat! I heard Nely Kick her back hoves and plod her front feet to the ground a little bit, but then she reconised me and gobbled the apple slice up. "Good girl," I said excited. Pits Pat! Pits Pat! She galloped away. "Good bye." I shouted. "What will she be up to?" I thought to myself. I can't wait to go back and feed Nely even more apple slices. Maybe I will even stay longer!

Notice, Name, and Note

Title of Piece/Author: "The Great Alpaca Ranch," by Lauren

Notice:
• Beautiful word choice

Name:
• Sensory language

Note: In addition to the focus and organization in this story, I am struck by the sensory language Lauren used: the crunching of gravel under her feet as she quickly walks to feed the alpaca; the snap of the apple slice as she breaks it in half; the wetness of the apple as it splashes her; the softness of the alpaca's lips as he takes the fruit from her hand; the pit-pat and plodding of the animal's front hooves as it recognizes her; and the sound of its hooves as it gallops away. This sensory language paints a beautiful picture for the reader.

"Treasure in the Garden" (Figure 1.5)

Recently I used Lauren's piece to teach a group of fourth graders about sensory language. A few days later Hadley told me that even though we were close to publishing (our celebration was only four days away), she wanted to start over: "I just feel I can do better." I encouraged her to revise her current piece, but she remained determined, and her home room teacher and I agreed to help her find the time to write a new story. For the next three days, Hadley spent every spare second (including recess) working on her writing. Her final draft, as well as her willingness to work so diligently on it, is one more example of the positive impact of student mentor texts.

Notice, Name, and Note

Title of Piece/Author: "Treasure in the Garden," by Hadley

Notice:
• Word choice

Name:
• Specific words
• Sound effects
• Figurative language
• Strong verbs

Note: Good writers write with specificity, and this is one of the biggest strengths of Hadley's piece. Wanting to describe her experience exactly, she chooses some very effective words. The sound effects that start a couple of paragraphs (*squish, squish* and *dig, dig*), the picture she paints of the garden at the beginning, the description of the hot shovel and the sun that she wishes she could hide with clouds, the description of the way she looked and felt after digging ("I was filthy from head to toe," "my arms were noodles"), and her excitement when she found the arrowhead ("I snatched it and stashed it away in my pocket") are just some of the things that make her language stand out.

Figure 1.5 Hadley, Fourth Grade, "Treasure in the Garden"

Hadley

Treasure In the garden

"Squish Squish", My feet sunk into the gooey garden pit. I was at my grandpa and grandma's farm. It was a perfect day for looking for arrow heads. It had just rained and the garden soil in between the veggies was rich in water. It sunk through the gaps in between your toes.

I got out a shiny shovle and a pair of green garden gloves. My fingers were slipery and the shovle was sizziling hot!!

Dig. dig. I was digging for an arrow head that was sharp around the edges and one I could fit in my pocket. My grandpa had a whole collection of arrow heads!! He said the best place to find arrow heads was right here in this verry garden.

Now the sun was realy shining. It was beating on my head. I wished I could just pull the clouds over the sun and make it dissapear. But It never

did what I wished. I kept on digging. By Then I was filthy from head to toe. I was about to give up. My clothes were loaded with dirt and my arms were noodles.

I gave one last dig. I sifted my hands through the dirt anxisly. Then I felt something unfamilur. It was sharp around the edges and small enough to fit in your pocket. It was an arrow head! I snatched it and stashed it away in my pocket.

I ran to the hose, Twisted the faucet and cleaned off my body and the arrow head.

Then I ran to the house. And said "Lookie here I have an arrow head", with a proud voice. My grandpa took it from my damp hand and inspected it. "You sure do, you sure do." "It's a pretty one too" The rest of the day that arrow head seemed to bring me good luck.

It was a treasure I would keep for ever and ever!

May be photocopied for classroom use. © 2015 by Lisa Eickholdt from *Learning from Classmates: Using Students' Writing as Mentor Texts*. Portsmouth, NH: Heinemann.

"A Horse and Some Hope" (Figure 1.6)

Aligning the instructional focus of various content areas is extremely helpful. When I am teaching students how to write informational pieces in writing workshop, I teach them how to read informational writing in reading workshop. And when science or social studies concepts are also integrated, things start to really make sense for kids. These fifth graders were studying the Great Depression during researchers' workshop (Stephanie Harvey [2014] suggests calling the daily social studies or science block *researcher's workshop* to reflect the inquiries students undertake), and their teacher was focusing on fiction from this period in both reading and writing workshop. Cassidy wrote a historical fiction piece about the Triple Crown–winning horse, Seabiscuit.

Notice, Name, and Note

Title of Piece/Author: "A Horse and Some Hope," by Cassidy

Notice:
• Historically accurate dialogue and details

Name:
• Historically accurate setting

Note: Writing fiction of any kind is difficult for most students. One challenge fiction writers face is creating believable characters. Writing historical fiction is an even greater challenge, because writers must create characters that are not only believable but also historically accurate. The character must behave in a way consistent with the period. One way writers accomplish this is to include authentic references to how the characters talk, dress, and live. The historically genuine setting is one of the things I find most impressive about this mentor text. Cassidy establishes the time period in various references.

• Through entertainment/technology: The story begins with the family entertaining themselves by sitting together listening to a horse race on the radio. At the end of the piece, as they drive to the race, most of the family is entertained by Dad's stories of serving in World War I, but Josephine is reading *Gone with the Wind*.
• Through living situation: The main character is one of a family of seven living in a small house. Money is tight—so tight, their mother asks them to turn off the radio to save electricity.
• Through transportation: The writer mentions roads recently built to accommodate all the Model Ts that "run, run, and run all day long." Additionally, the main character walks to the local store to fill out the raffle ticket. The images of the local store with its old World War I propaganda poster ("that nobody bothered to take down"), the "ding-a-ling-ling" of the store's door as she enters, and the counter full of penny candy and other small items all transport the reader back to another era.

Figure 1.6 Cassidy, Fifth Grade, "A Horse and Some Hope"

A Horse and Some Hope by Cassidy H. 3/3/1940

"And they're off with Seabiscuit in the lead! They zip around the first bend and..." Crckzzzck. The race announcer's voice fizzles out as Mom turns the radio off.

"Come on guys, you know you're using too much electricity listening to race after race," Mom scolds. "You all know how tough this Great Depression is!"

"But Mommy, Seabiscuit was racing!" my brother, Leo, complains in his whiny seven-year-old voice.

A chorus of "yeah's" and "uh-huh's" ring through-out the den as Lily, Hunter, Leo, Josephina, and I protest Mom.

Yeah, I know. We've got a houseful, which just makes money more scarce during these tough times.

Once Mom leaves the room, we sit in an awkward silence. All of the sudden, Lily blurts out, "I want to watch Seabiscuit race in real life!" She can't help it; she's only four. The impossible dream hangs in the air, and we all know we want to see that amazing horse race too.

I yearn to see a horse race live more than any of the others, and I've always wanted to be a jockey even more. I'm light, nimble, and small, a perfect fit for the job. But my problem is the same as everyone's problem: the Great Depression.

A couple of days later, while I'm walking our skimpy beagle down the streets of southern California, I hear a group of migrant workers talking excitedly outside of a soup kitchen.

"Can you believe it?!" one of them exclaims. "A chance to watch Seabiscuit race live! All we need to do is enter some drawing and we could win 7 tickets for the Santa Anita!"

Wow, I think to myself. Wow, wow, wow! A chance of a life-time, and all I need to do is enter a raffle! It seems too good to be true!

I sprint across the new road that was built for all those Model T's that run, run, run all day long. Once I ask the migrant workers where the drawing is, they point me to the corner store.

I race there, dragging along my dog, Sadie, on her leash. I glance at the old World War I propaganda posters that nobody bothered to take down from the store's windows, and then push the door open.

Ding-a-ling-ling! The store's bell rings as I walk inside. I dash over to the clerk's counter full of candy and other small treats and fill out a raffle card. "Mia Williams, age 13," I write quickly and drop the card in the raffle box. Now, I just have to wait.

"MOM! MOM! MOM!" I scream as I bolt into the house a day later. "I won! I won! I won!" I waved the seven lucky tickets in the air.

I had been stopped on the street by the store owner and was given the precious tickets, so I ran home as fast as one of those new airplanes to spread the amazing news!

Now, my family swarmed around me, clambering over the lucky tickets. Hunter snatched one out of my hand and asked, "Is it real?"

"It sure is!" Josephina, my older sister, replies, pushing her long, dark hair out of her eyes as she reads the tickets. "Santa Anita, March 2nd, 1940. One admission."

I couldn't believe our luck! This moment was better than Christmas, my birthday, and all the money in the world mixed together! I wanted to explode with happiness and excitement!

The next few days were full of tension and thrill. The whole family went shopping to replace our dirty, ragged clothes with nicer ones, and I had to brush and brush my long,

auburn hair.

Finally, FINALLY, the big day was here! Just as the sun's rays started to turn the night sky pink and gold, I awoke groggily. Then it hits me! The race is today! I jump out of bed like a spring and throw on my new clothes. "Mia!" my dad calls, "Come on and get in the car!"

He didn't need to tell me twice. As fast as you can say "Franklin Delanor Roosevelt," I'm down the stairs and out the door. Then, I sprint down the dirt driveway and scramble into our family's Model T.

It's a long and grueling ride to the racetrack. Josephina wants peace and quiet so she can read "Gone With the Wind", but Hunter and Leo want to listen to Dad's stories about serving in World War I. Lily sleeps most of the way, and I just daydream about Seabiscuit and being a jockey.

After what seems like a million years, we pull up to the biggest, and, well, only, stadium I've ever seen. Swarms of fans are flooding through the big door, and the smells of horses, potato fries, and funnel cakes are overwhelming. The whole family scrambles out of the car, tired of eachother, and Hunter and Leo run straight to the entrance with Lily toddling after them.

"Welcome, ladies and gentlemen, to the 1940 Santa Anita!" the announcer exclaims over the loudspeaker as we plop down in our seats. The roar of about 70,000 fans was deafening, and Lily covers her ears with her hands. "I know many of you are here to see the famous Seabiscuit," the announcer continues. The roar is even louder at the mention of the famous horse's name.

"And, without further ado," the man announces, "Let the race begin!"

TWEET! A shrill whistle blows and they're off! Automatically, my eyes are drawn to Seabiscuit and his jockey, Red Pollard. They don't look like much. Seabiscuit's run is wobbly and off-balance, and Red is just recovering from a hurt leg.

The mass of horses turned the first bend at a lightning speed with Seabiscuit trailing behind a couple of other horses, one of them Kayak II, a super fast race horse.

"Go, Seabiscuit, go!" I holler as I jump up and down in the crowd. I stand on my tippy-toes to see as the horses race past the halfway mark. Ever so slowly, Seabiscuit gains speed and passes one, no two, other horses! He's in second, right behind... ergh... Kayak II.

"Come on 'Biscuit!" my dad yells in his booming voice. "You can do it!"

The mob of horses passes by our seats in a blur, but not too quickly because I can see the look of determination on Red Pollard's face.

Suddenly, Red urges Seabiscuit to go faster and faster! The stadium roars like a wild animal, but I'm holding my breath.

Now, the 'Biscuit and Kayak II are neck-and-neck on the home stretch! The world blurs, and I feel as if it's in slow motion. Each stride of the horses seems to take a year, but slowly and surely, Seabiscuit takes the lead!

"YES! YES!" I scream in joy as Seabiscuit passes Kayak II with flying colors and soars across the finish line like a free bird. When I see Red's smiling face, I know right then and there that I definitely want to be a jockey.

25 YEARS LATER

Bam! Bam! Bam! Dirt flies as I grip onto the mane of my horse, and I hear the screams and cheers of the stadium around me. My hair flies out of my jockey helmet, flapping crazily in the wind. Some people don't like me, a woman, be a jockey, but Seabiscuit proved that anyone could be strong. I just have to believe!

Poetry Samples

Almost every student can write wonderful poems if encouraged to write free verse poetry (Heard 1999). Because poems are often short, students who struggle with volume find this genre less demanding and it often becomes one of their favorite forms of writing.

"Goodbye" (Figure 1.7)

Gracie wrote this poem during a historical fiction unit of study after her book club had read several books about the Vietnam War and the class had spent a couple of weeks reading and discussing this conflict. She wrote the poem from the perspective of a soldier. Gracie came up with this idea on her own, but asking students to write from a different point of view or "through a mask" (Portalupi and Fletcher 1998) is a great way to integrate writing into the content areas.

Figure 1.7 Gracie, Fifth Grade, "Goodbye"

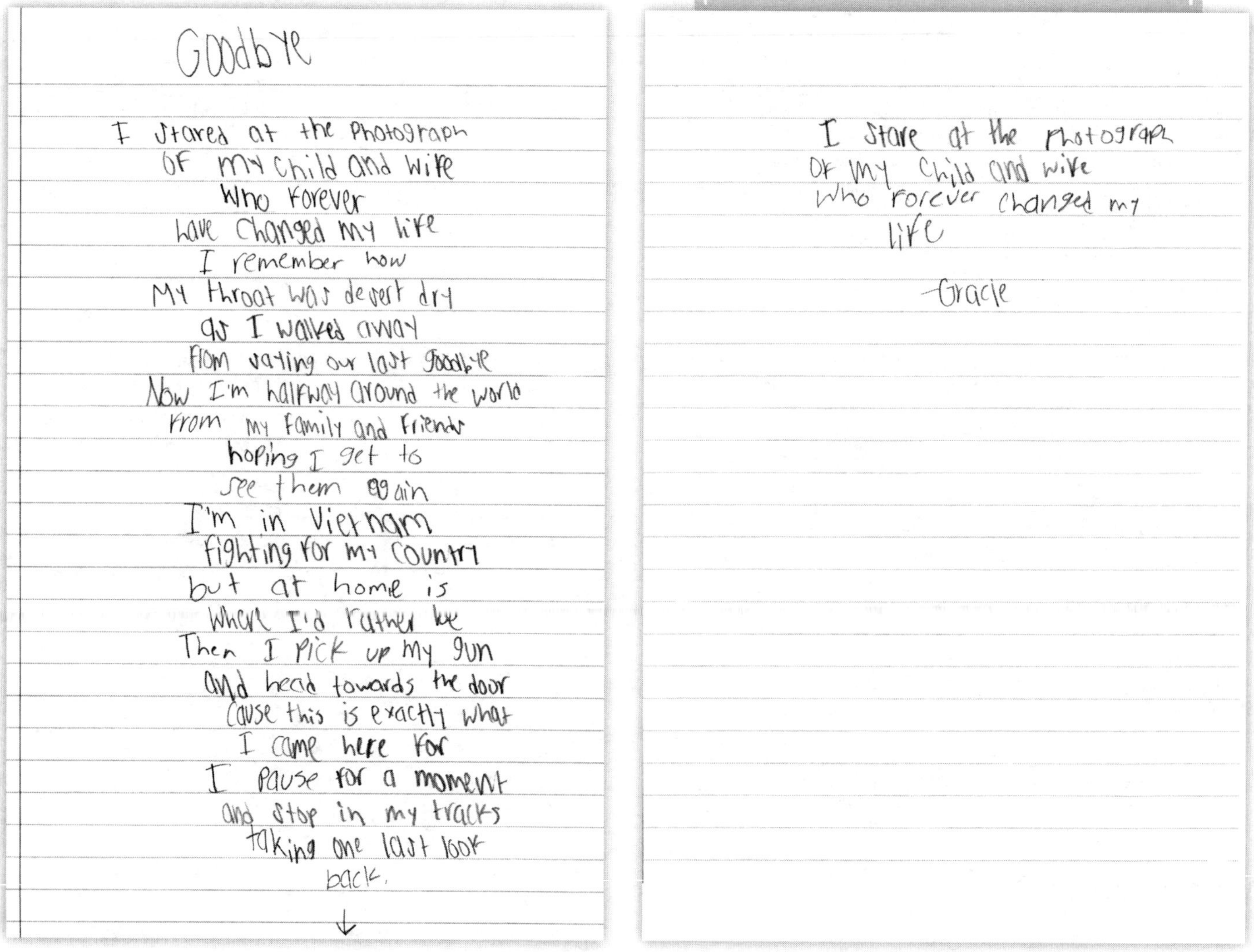

Goodbye

I stared at the photograph
of my child and wife
Who forever
have changed my life
I remember how
My throat was desert dry
as I walked away
from saying our last goodbye
Now I'm halfway around the world
from my family and friends
hoping I get to
see them again
I'm in Vietnam
fighting for my country
but at home is
where I'd rather be
Then I pick up my gun
and head towards the door
cause this is exactly what
I came here for
I pause for a moment
and stop in my tracks
taking one last look
back.
↓

I stare at the photograph
of my child and wife
who forever changed my
life

Gracie

Notice, Name, and Note

Title of Piece/Author: "Goodbye," by Gracie

Notice:
• Image of the soldier staring at a photo of his family

Name:
• Imagery and emotion

Note: Poems are built around one or more "pillars of poetry" (Portalupi and Fletcher 2004): imagery, emotion, and music (rhythm). Gracie's poem possesses all three (not every poem does nor should), but the imagery stands out. Gracie does a beautiful job of weaving a family photograph throughout the piece. This image is planted at the start of the poem when we see the young soldier staring at the photograph as he flashes back to their last good-bye. Gracie wisely repeats this image in the last stanza, leaving us with a picture of the soldier looking back at his family one last time on his way out to battle. This final impression makes the reader wonder whether this will be the soldier's last good-bye.

The imagery adds to the emotion generated by the poem. The photograph makes us feel the homesickness and loneliness that many soldiers feel. Gracie also alludes to the soldier's fear of death in the third stanza when she writes, "Now I'm halfway around the world / from my family and friends / hoping I get to / see them again." Finally, we sense the soldier's bravery. We know he's afraid, yet we watch him do what he feels is his duty for his country. His courage comes through when we see him grab his gun and head off to battle "Cause this is exactly / what I came here for." Because poems are so short, a writer must carefully choose each and every word. Gracie's thoughtful word choices trigger a myriad of emotions.

"Hug Me, Daddy" (Figure 1.8)

I found this poem when I was working in a third grade classroom. Ashlyn was trying to convey the love between herself and her father. Earlier in the year, we had learned to use actions to show, rather than tell, how characters are feeling in narrative writing. Ashlyn wisely applied this same writing technique to her poem.

Figure 1.8 Ashlyn, Third Grade, "Hug Me, Daddy"

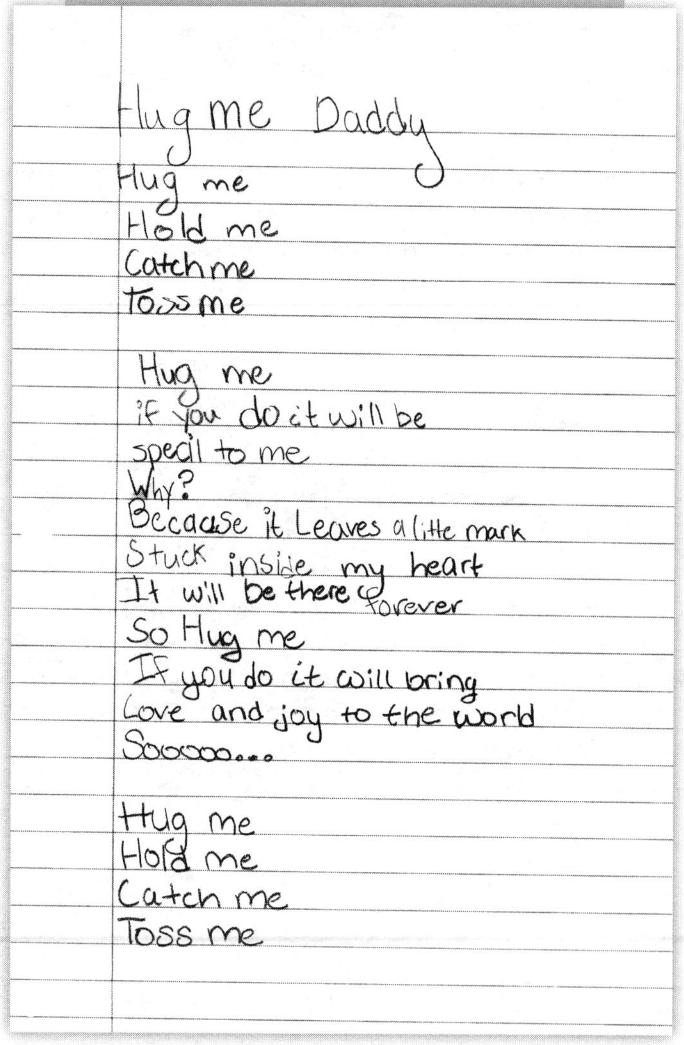

Hug me Daddy
Hug me
Hold me
Catch me
Toss me

Hug me
if you do it will be
speal to me
Why?
Because it Leaves a litte mark
Stuck inside my heart
It will be there forever
So Hug me
If you do it will bring
Love and joy to the world
Soooooo...

Hug me
Hold me
Catch me
Toss me

Notice, Name, and Note

Title of Piece/Author: "Hug Me, Daddy," by Ashlyn

Notice:
• Strong feeling and rhythm

Name:
• Emotion and music

Note: This poem has many things to offer, but what stands out most is the emotion. The warm feeling I get every time I read it makes me smile. Ashlyn writes about the power a father's hug can have on a child, telling him that his affection "leaves a little mark / stuck inside my heart." I also appreciate the music. One of the ways Ashlyn creates rhythm is by beginning and ending with the same stanza. These "bookends" are a form of repetition, and repetition is a great way to add music to poetry.

"The Beach" (Figure 1.9)

I encountered the following poem in a class of second graders. When the classroom teacher and I began the unit, we immersed the students in poetry. One of the things the kids noticed was that many poems are written about things in nature. M. J. wrote this poem soon after reading some poems about the natural world. I love the images he creates. He was very excited when I told him I was going to use his poem in my lesson. To this day, every time I see him in the hallway, he smiles and says, "Hey, it's me! Your favorite poet!" And he's right!

Notice, Name, and Note

Title of Piece/Author: "The Beach," by M. J.

Notice:
• I feel like I am at the beach.

Name:
• Personification

Note: This poem contains strong imagery. Ways poets create imagery include using figurative language like similes, metaphors, and personification. M. J. does a wonderful job of using personification. I particularly admire how different aspects of the beach show him affection. The ocean tickling his feet, the sun kissing his face, and the waves hugging him tight all convey his happiness at and love for being at the beach, feelings most of us share.

The Beach

MJ

when I get to the Beach
The wind blows
MY facs
The ocean tickls
mr feet
the sun kissis
my facs
the sand srachis
MY leggs
the wavs hug
me tite
the seegols sing
Me a song
When I get to th beach

Opinion/Argumentative Writing Samples

Kids are prone to debate. When we tell a child no, he or she usually tries to convince
us to change our mind. Kids like to defend their opinion and argue their point. We
can capitalize on this natural inclination by including units of study on opinion and
argumentative writing.

Junie B. Jones *Book Review (Figure 1.10)*

This book review always makes me laugh! My favorite part is when Megan writes
about her friend's reaction to learning that candy corn is not a vegetable—too funny!
I use this piece as a model for how to incorporate voice into nonnarrative writing,
something that is often hard for kids to do.

Figure 1.10 Megan, Third Grade, *Junie B. Jones* Book Review

Are you a scardy-cat-baby about Halloween? I'm not, but Junie B. Jones is! Junie B. First Grader BOO...and I MEAN IT! is one of the many hilarious books by Barbara Park.

Tomarrow is Halloween, and Junie B. Jones is panicking! Well, wouldn't you be nervous if you knew five scary secrets about Halloween? Sorry, I can't tell you them or my head will turn into a wart, possibly. Just kidding. Anyways, in this book Junie B. is trying to find a way to pervent herself from going trick-or-treating. Will Mother make her go? Is Junie B. going to tell the secrets? Is her head going to turn into a wart? Will my head turn into a wart? Find all the answers in this book. Well except for the last one.

This book reminds me of when I was in first grade. My friend and I were debating over the fact that candy corn is not corn. When I told her, she was very shocked.

Junie B. Jones books are hilarious books to read. But her series isn't the only series Barbara Park has written. If you have ever read a Skinny Bones book, then you will love Junie B. First Grader BOO...and I MEAN IT!

Barbara Park is a truly silly writer. She's like Junie B.'s big sister! Every single book she has written I have read, and liked. Once you read her books you will be hooked.

Notice, Name, and Note

Title of Piece/Author: *Junie B. Jones* Book Review, by Megan

Notice:
• I feel like the writer is talking directly to me.

Name:
• Voice

Note: Ways Megan incorporates voice into her piece include talking directly to the reader ("Sorry I can't tell you them or my head will turn into a wart, possibly. Just kidding."); asking the reader questions ("Will mother make her go? Is Junie B. going to tell the secrets? Is her head going to turn into a wart? Will my head turn into a wart?"); answering questions ("I'm not, but Junie B. Jones is"); and adding an afterthought ("Well, except for the last one."). These are all specific writing techniques that students can use to make their writing have a stronger voice.

Lin's Bistro Restaurant Review (Figure 1.11)

One of my favorite ways to teach opinion writing is through a unit on reviews. Students can review their favorite books, video games, apps, movies, music, or restaurants. Kids love to share their opinions. Posting students' final reviews at the library, local restaurants, or gaming stores, as appropriate, provides a great culmination to this unit. Merchants are usually more than happy to display these for all to see!

Notice, Name, and Note

Title of Piece/Author: Lin's Bistro Restaurant Review, by Eva

Notice:
• Where to find the restaurant
• Description of the way the restaurant looks
• Menu items
• Comparison and recommendation

Name:
• Parts of a restaurant review

Note: Though all reviews are alike because they are opinion pieces, every type of review has its own structure. Creating anchor charts (Angelillo 2003; Taylor and Calkins 2008) for each type helps students understand how to organize them. The students and I read a few examples of each type of review, then list and name the sections we notice. These anchor charts remain up throughout the unit so students can refer to them as they write and decide what parts they will (or will not) include in their piece. Eva's sections on the décor and menu are unique to restaurant reviews. Examining how she structures her piece can be helpful to other students.

Figure 1.11 Eva, Second Grade, Lin's Bistro Restaurant Review

Title Lin's Bistro

Reviewer Eva

 Me

 My Best Friend at lin's bistro. But I have lots of other friends too.

If you like chinese food, then Lin's Bistro is the restraunt for you. I like it alot because I have friends that work there and I get to see people cook. Lins Bistro is off Braselton Highway in Lawrenceville. Lin's Bistro looks a little like a chinese palace or temple to me.

It is very instresting because every time I walk in it makes me feel like I'm in china. It also makes me feel lik I'm in my grand parent's house becayse of all the Korean decorations.

  white rice soup Fried rice Lo main

On the menu are tons of things to choose from I can't name all, but I can name my 3 favorites: chicken fried rice, won ton soup, and Lo main. I like chiken fried rice because theres alot of chiken, rice, and veggies. I like wonton soup because there are alot of chicken dumplings in it. My parents buy me the chicken lomain alot but not as much as chicken fried rice. I like lomain because there are lots of chinese noodles and other healthy thing for us. Even though there is not a kids menu they are really nice to them.

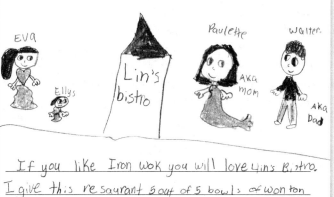 Eva Ellys Lin's bistro Paulette aka mom Walter. aka Dad

If you like Iron wok you will love Lin's Bistro. I give this resaurant 5 out of 5 bowls of won ton soup (ᴗᴗᴗᴗᴗ). I say ages one through one hundred should eat here.

"Sweet Dreams for a Bunk Bed" (Figure 1.12)

In this letter Cassidy uses reasons and examples to make the point that she needs a bunk bed. Her piece is also filled with voice. The combination of sound persuasive techniques and a strong voice creates a very convincing piece. A couple of years after Cassidy wrote this letter, I saw her and her mom at a local park. Cassidy eagerly waved me over, saying she had some important news. As I approached she yelled, "I got a bunk bed for Christmas!" The power of the pen!

Notice, Name, and Note

Title of Piece/Author: "Sweet Dreams for a Bunk Bed," by Cassidy

Notice:
• I can hear Cassidy talking to me!

Name:
• Voice

Note: Like the *Junie B. Jones* book review, this letter is filled with voice. Cassidy uses several writing techniques to integrate her voice into her writing. She talks directly to the reader—in this case, her mom and dad—asking and answering questions: "Remember when you told me that when you were a kid you wanted a bunk bed? Well, I'm in the same situation right now." "You want more? Sure you do." She also uses parentheses to help create an image—"(huffing-puffing, huffing, puffing)"— to show what she is thinking—"(hint-hint)"—and to add information—"(one on top of the other)." Together these techniques create a humorous, sweet, convincing note.

Figure 1.12 Cassidy, Third Grade, "Sweet Dreams for a Bunk Bed"

Sweet Dreams For A Bunk-Bed

Dear Mommy and Daddy,

Hey Mommy, remember when you told me that when you were a kid you wanted a bunk-bed? Well I'm in the same situation right NOW! I want a bunk-bed and I want it bad! You might not give it to me now but I'm pretty sure you will after you read all my reasons why I really want a bunk-bed!

(Huffing, puffing, huffing, puffing.) Isn't it tiring blowing up the air mattress every single time I have a sleepover? If I had a bunk-bed (hint-hint) all your troubles would be gone! Plus, have you noticed some of my friends don't even like sleeping on the air matteress? For me it is hard to sleep without my radio, so how am I supposed to listen to it if I'm sleeping in the playroom and it's sitting as still as a stump on my dresser?!?! You want more? Sure you do! Read on for more reasons why I need a bunk-bed!

You've probably noticed that Daniel sleeps half the night in your room! And in YOUR BED?!?! If you go and get me a bunk-bed all your troubles disappear the moment the bunk-bed gets set down in my room. Daniel would come in my bed because I would have two. (One on top of the other.) I wouldn't even notice! Also, if someone had to stay at our house and sleep in Daniel's room he could sleep on the bottom bunk of my bunk-bed. I know you don't want to think like this, but what if the terrible, horrible, and ugly ants come back and somehow wiggle their way back into Daniel's room? I'm pretty sure Daniel would not want to sleep in a room infested with ants. I know I wouldn't. Have you decided YET?!?! If you haven't read on. I think I know what your answer will be. ☺

A bunk-bed is not only cool, it's handy, too! If you look at my bulliten board you can see I'm starting to have to overlap pictures and papers. If I had a bunk-bed I could hang things on the side of it. (But not my wet towel, of course.) Plus, have you noticed that my pillows and stuffed animals sometimes fall of my bed? If I got a bunk-bed all those problems would poof away. I would have TWO beds to put that stuff on. Isn't a bunk-bed great? Also if Daniel's being as wild as a two year old, as hyper as a duck on caffenie, and as jumpy as a kangaroo, I can get some well needed rest on my top bunk. He wouldn't be able to reach me if I moved the ladder. (But since Daniel is so nice that would hardly happen, but it's nice to be prepeared.) Keep reading to make your final decision!

Have you changed your mind? Have you decided yes?!?! Don't you think your loving, caring, sweet daughter should have her very own bunk-bed? If you say no you each have to write me a five-paragraph essay on why I shouldn't have a bunk-bed!

Love your caring kid,
Cassidy H. (#4)

(P.S. If you say no I'll still love you, but if you say yes I'll love you even more!)

Things to keep in mind ----------------------------

Immersion

* Expose students to the genre: Immerse students before they write by reading lots of great mentor texts. This activity will give them a sense of the genre.

* Chart it: Work with students to highlight the key features of a genre. Post these on a class anchor chart.

* Choose wisely: Choose mentor texts that are filled with great craft so you can return to these same texts over and over again for different teaching points.

* Give a copy: Provide students with a copy of the mentor text to store in their writing folders. They can then return to the text over and over again as they are writing.

* Name it: Be sure to name the writing technique for students. Remember, naming something makes it repeatable.

* Don't assume compliance: Just because you tell students to do something, don't assume they will. Instead, help students understand why they should use a certain writing technique. Explain why it's effective. Show students how it will help them as writers or how it improves their writing.

Assessment

Making Sure to Evaluate
Your Students' Needs

> Assessment is the thinking teacher's mind work. It is the
> intelligence that guides our every moment as a teacher.
>
> —*Lucy Calkins*

Assessment informs what we do as teachers. It prompts us to reflect on students' responses to our instruction. When we work with kids each day, we constantly assess their reactions to our teaching and use this information to make changes to our lessons. According to Calkins (2013), "The research is clear that the one factor that matters more than anything in determining whether students' levels of achievement accelerate is the quality of your teaching. You need to teach responsively" (3). There are many ways and reasons to assess. This chapter focuses on assessment that helps us find student writing to use as a mentor text. I'll describe the process first and then share an example of how the process is applied in the classroom.

ASSESSING STUDENT WRITING TO INFORM WHOLE-GROUP INSTRUCTION

In addition to assessing individual students' writing each day as you confer, it is also helpful to periodically assess your group of writers. Examining your group's writing enables you to plan future lessons, create small groups, and find student writing which may be used as mentor texts. One way to make sure whole group assessments guide our instruction is to make them more systematic. Knowing that we will assess our whole group of writers before, during, and after any unit we teach ensures that our instruction is responsive.

Step 1: Gathering

You can use a couple of ways to gather your students' writing to assess them as a group. One is to ask students to complete a short response or on-demand writing (Calkins 2013). Another is to ask students to hand in their writing folders or notebooks, then assess either process or content. If you wonder whether students understand the writing process, skim through a few samples with process in mind. If you're concerned about genre or craft, ask students to write a quick response, or skim their writing looking for a specific writing quality.

Step 2: Searching

As you read through each student's writing, search for patterns. In addition to noticing all the things your students already know about writing well, identify key writing concepts that most of your students need help with. The instructional decisions you make should be influenced by what you believe about good writing.

Many teachers are initially unclear about what it means to write well. Most of us grew up in a time when writing was assigned and evaluated but rarely taught. If our teachers did provide feedback, it was often regarding conventions and came from a red pen. Having had no instruction on how to improve content ourselves, we often struggle to teach our students how to write well. Fortunately, plenty of professional resources can help you define the qualities of powerful writing.

One is *Teaching the Qualities of Writing*, by JoAnn Portalupi and Ralph Fletcher (2004). This book discusses the qualities the authors believe are most important to good writing: ideas, design, language, and presentation. Vicki Spandel, along with a group of educators (Spandel 2001; Culham 2003), created a list of six traits, widely known as the six-trait writing assessment (sometimes 6+1), that they consider essential to writing well. These traits, which are the basis for many assessment rubrics, are ideas, organization, voice, word choice, sentence structure, fluency, and conventions/layout. (In the 6 + 1 designation, the seventh trait is presentation.) Because of their widespread use, these traits have helped define what good writing looks like for many teachers. Other valuable resources are those created by Lucy Calkins and her colleagues at the Teachers College Reading and Writing Project (TCRWP). Their units of study for teaching writing are filled with excellent lessons on various writing techniques.

Step 3: Sorting

As you read each child's writing, use all you know about good writing to sort your students' work. Many qualities are associated with good writing. In addition to understanding them, it helps to pinpoint the traits you believe are the most important and rank them. Every writing trait should not receive the same degree of attention; some traits are more important to teach because of the impact they have on students' writing as a whole.

The qualities I believe are most helpful to student writers are:

- meaning/focus
- structure
- elaboration/details
- craft
- conventions.

Because I believe these traits are essential, they are the first things I look for when I assess my students' writing. If one of these qualities is missing, I'll include lessons on it in my instructional plans.

Meaning/Focus

Because it is so important, meaning is the first trait listed on most assessment rubrics. It could include things like adhering to the characteristics of the genre and elaborating, but I place these attributes under other qualities. The most important thing about meaning to me is focus. A focused piece of writing is clear, coherent, and about one key idea. Questions to consider when sorting student writing based on meaning include the following:

- Is the student writing about one small moment, event, or idea?
- Am I able to determine the writer's message?

Structure

After I determine that a piece is focused, I check to see how well it's structured. A well-structured piece adheres to the characteristics of the genre. For example, a narrative should have a beginning, middle, and end; an essay has a thesis statement supported with main ideas and details. The structure of a piece directly impacts the meaning. To have a well-structured piece, the writer needs to determine what events or details to include or exclude to tell the story or make the point. For grades 3 through 12, the Common Core State Standards address structure in writing standard 4: Students should "produce clear and coherent writing in which the development and organization are appropriate to task, purpose, and audience" (18). Questions to consider when sorting student writing based on structure include the following:

- Are students including key elements of the genre?
- Are students including the most important events or factors?
- Are students excluding extraneous events or factors?
- Are students grouping their ideas in meaningful ways?
- Are students drawing readers in with their lead and wrapping things up with their ending?

Elaboration/Details

A strongly elaborated piece is more meaningful because details make an idea clearer. Much of what we teach students is some form of elaboration. Adding thoughts or feelings, dialogue, and specific action are ways to elaborate a narrative. Adding anecdotes, numerical data, and research can elaborate nonnarrative pieces. In *What a Writer Needs* (1993), Ralph Fletcher says, "Writing becomes beautiful when it becomes specific" (47). Specificity has a lot to do with language and word choice, with describing things using small, precise details. When students start using precise language, strong verbs and specific nouns naturally begin to show up in their writing. Questions to consider when sorting student writing based on elaboration/details include the following:

- Are students elaborating important scenes or stances?
- Are students using specific details?

Craft

A finely crafted piece of writing gives the sense that the writer is not just recounting a story or making a point but also trying to help the reader envision and enjoy the piece. Adding sensory language builds imagery. Adding similes and metaphors helps readers visualize a situation or the setting. Varying sentence length can help the writer make a point or add a lyrical quality. Questions to consider when sorting student writing based on craft include the following:

- Are students writing in a way that will help the reader envision or enjoy the writing more (audience awareness)?
- Are students using figurative or sensory language?

Conventions

Conventions are at the bottom of my list of writing qualities, but not because I don't teach my students how to use conventions; I do. It's just that there is so much to teach students about improving the content of their writing that conventions aren't my priority. This quotation from the NCTE website encapsulates the struggle between teaching content and conventions:

> Every teacher has to resolve a tension between writing as generating and shaping ideas and writing as demonstrating expected surface conventions. On the one hand, it is important for writing to be as correct as possible and for students to be able to produce correct texts. On the other hand, achieving correctness is only one set of things writers must be able to do; a correct text empty of ideas or unsuited to its audience or purpose is not a good piece of writing. (http://www .ncte.org/positions/statements/writingbeliefs)

We have all read student pieces that are "empty of ideas or unsuited to their purpose"; this serious concern warrants and should receive priority. Questions to consider when sorting student writing based on conventions include the following:

- Are students using all they know about spelling words?
- Are students using internal and external punctuation?
- Are students using punctuation to add meaning to their writing?

See Figure 2.1 for more.

Figure 2.1 Questions to Consider When Sorting Students' Writing

Meaning/Focus

- Is the student writing about one small moment, event, or idea?
- Am I able to determine the writer's message?

Structure

- Are students including key elements of the genre?
- Are students including the most important events or factors?
- Are students excluding extraneous events or factors?
- Are students grouping their ideas in meaningful ways?
- Are students drawing readers in with their lead and wrapping things up with their ending?

Elaboration/Details

- Are students elaborating important scenes or stances?
- Are students using specific details?

Craft

- Are students writing in a way that will help the reader envision or enjoy the writing more (audience awareness)?
- Are students using figurative or sensory language?

Conventions

- Are students using all they know about spelling to spell words?
- Are students using internal and external punctuation?
- Are students using punctuation to add meaning to their writing?

Step 4: Deciding

As you read each child's writing, searching for what he or she needs help with, briefly jot notes about what you notice. Clear themes will emerge—for example, perhaps you've written *leads* on your list of things students need help with, and the list of names underneath is growing long. Searching and sorting through your students' writing helps you decide what to focus your teaching around. Set a few teaching goals each time you assess the group, and use them to guide your teaching. When most of your students have met these goals, reassess and set new ones.

The form in Figure 2.2 helps you organize this process. Jot down the writing qualities you think are the most pressing, and list each student who needs to work on that quality. In the box adjacent to each quality, record the names of students whose writing can be used as a mentor text. For example, if most of your students seem to need help with paragraphing, but a few students already understand the concept, invite these "paragraphing experts" to mentor the others.

Figure 2.2 Whole-Group Assessment and Sorting Sheet

UNIT:			DATE:
Writing Quality: Students:	Student Mentor Text:	Writing Quality: Students:	Student Mentor Text:
Writing Quality: Students:	Student Mentor Text:	Writing Quality: Students:	Student Mentor Text:
Writing Quality: Students:	Student Mentor Text:	Writing Quality: Students:	Student Mentor Text:

WRITING GOALS/LESSONS:

1.

2.

3.

4.

This assessment also helps you determine how to deliver your instruction. If many students need help with a particular writing quality, you'll teach a whole-class lesson. If only a few kids need help with a particular writing technique, however, you can teach it to just this small group. Figure 2.3 is a completed assessment and sorting sheet for a fourth-grade class.

Step 5: Teaching

Once you determine what instructional help your students need, you will then need to decide how to teach. Every child, no matter how young, can learn to improve the content of her or his writing, but you'll need to adjust your teaching according to your students' age and level of development. The younger and less experienced the writer, the simpler your instruction. During a writing lesson you can use student writing, your own writing, or a piece of children's literature as a mentor text. In every unit of study, students should encounter each of these models. The planning guide in Figure 2.4 helps you determine how you will help students meet the goals you've set. (Figure 2.5 is an example of a completed lesson planning guide for a fourth-grade class.)

Figure 2.3 Completed Assessment and Sorting Sheet, Fourth-Grade Class

Whole Group Assessment and Sorting Sheet

Unit: Information Essays - 4th grade   Date: 10|18

Writing Quality: Focus Kids who need help with this:	Student Mentor Text:	Writing Quality: Overall Organization Kids who need help with this:	Student Mentor Text:
Travis Courtney Olivia Ryan Caleb Reggie Sam Lillie Cammy Connor Chris Henry	Cameron Lauren Nick Jackson Ryan	Chris Riley Olivia Reggie Caleb Henry Sam Alex Cammy Jordan Courtney Tracy Ryan Mary	Cameron Lauren Jackson Lillie Ryan
Writing Quality: Internal Organization Kids who need help with this:	Student Mentor Text:	Writing Quality: Kids who need help with this:	Student Mentor Text:
Travis Mary Caleb Ryan Cameron Jackson Cammy Riley Jordan Chris Tracy	Olivia Eva Sam Reggie		
Writing Quality: Kids who need help with this:	Student Mentor Text:	Writing Quality: Kids who need help with this:	Student Mentor Text:

Writing Goals and lessons based on this data:

1. Focus
2. Overall structure
3. Within paragraph structure
4. _____

Figure 2.4 Lesson Planning Guide

UNIT:	DATE:

WRITING GOALS/LESSONS:

WRITING GOAL/QUALITY	TEACHING METHODS/LESSONS

Figure 2.5 Completed Lesson Planning Sheet, Fourth-Grade Class

Lesson Planning Sheet

Unit: Informational Essays—4th   Dates: 10/21 – 10/25

Writing Goals:
Focus, overall organization, internal organization

Writing Goal/Quality	Teaching Methods/Lessons
- Zoom in & focus in informational like in narrative.	Student Mentor Text: - Nick - Lauren
Ways to organize an essay (reasons, kinds)	- My writing
Ways to organize an essay (parts, ways, times)	- My writing - Time for Kids Article
Organizing writing w/in paragraphs (main idea/details)	Student Mentor Text: Sam
Elaborating with transitions (use sentence stems).	Student Mentor Text: Logan

A Classroom Example

I was recently invited to help launch writing workshop in Debbie McMichael's second-grade classroom. We began with a unit on personal narrative writing.

Preassessment

During the first week of school, Deb gives her students forty-five minutes to write their best small-moment story. We then examine these stories, looking for trends, particularly in relation to focus, structure, and elaboration. The results are shown in Figure 2.6.

Figure 2.6 Preassessment of a Second-Grade Class's Initial Writing Needs

Whole Group Assessment and Sorting Sheet

Unit: Personal Narrative   Date: 8/18/13

Writing Quality: Focus Kids who need help with this:	Student Mentor Text:	Writing Quality: Inner Story Kids who need help with this:	Student Mentor Text:
Kelly Jo Chase Hayden Isabelle } Most kids Tyler Kathryn Loan Bryan Ashley Morgan Trevor maddie	Nicole Luke Connor Brandon	Kelly Jo Chase Hayden Isabelle } Most kids Tyler Kathryn Ashley Bryan Trevor Morgan	Loan Jaden Nicole Luke Connor Brandon
Writing Quality: Specific Actions Kids who need help with this:	Student Mentor Text:	**Writing Quality: Pacing** Kids who need help with this:	Student Mentor Text:
Kelly Jo Chase Hayden Isabelle Tyler Kathryn Loan Bryan Ashley Trevor } Most	None	Hayden Tyler	
Writing Quality: Story Structure Kids who need help with this:	Student Mentor Text:	Writing Quality: Kids who need help with this:	Student Mentor Text:
Matthew (diff. story on each pg) Brynne Marie Isabelle } Tell stories across pages Maddie - Write about what you remember			

Writing Goals/Minilessons based on this data:

1. Focus / Small Moment
2. Elaborate with inner story
3. Elaborate with specific actions
4. _____

Most students' initial writing sounds something like this:

One day I went to my friend's house to go swimming. We hopped in the car and drove to my friend's house. When I got there, I went inside and got on my bathing suit. Then, I went outside to the pool and went swimming. Then we got out of the pool. I went upstairs and took a shower. We went to bed and I went to sleep. Then, I woke up and played for three hours and mom came to get me. I hopped in the car and we drove home.

These young writers believe telling a story means recounting everything that happened to them from the time they woke up to the time they went to sleep.

To help them focus their writing, we decide to teach them how to write a small-moment story (Calkins and Oxenhorn 2003)—a highly focused personal narrative about one meaningful event (that usually takes place in twenty minutes or less). Narrowing the time span a child writes about immediately improves the focus of the piece. Figure 2.7 is the lesson planning guide we created. Although most of the kids need help with focus, several do not. These students become mentors for our first lesson.

The same is true with regard to elaborating a story by going inside (Calkins and Oxenhorn 2003)—telling what the characters are thinking. A few students tell how they are feeling in their pieces. Though these examples are very basic, we use them as a model. Most writers' initial attempts at any technique will be basic, and we want the work to seem achievable to even the most struggling writers. Also, this lesson is just the first in a series in which we gradually introduce more complex ways to get inside the story. We use all three modeling methods: student writing, my writing, and children's literature.

Lesson Planning Sheet

Unit: Personal Narrative 2nd grade   Dates: 8/19 – 8/23

Writing Goals: Focus & Elaboration

Writing Goal/Quality	Teaching Methods/Lessons
Focus / small moment	Student Mentor Text: Nicole Connor Luke Brandon
Focus / small moment	My writing: Park story Before/after lesson
Elaborate using inside story.	Student Mentor Text: Brandon & Luke
Elaborate using inside story.	My writing - add into park story.
Elaborate using specific actions-What are your hands, feet, eyes doing?	Children's Literature: Fireflies by Brinckloe

Figure 2.7 Lesson Plan to Address Preassessed Writing Needs

Gathering and Searching Through Drafts

Once most of the students have met the initial writing goals we've set—at the unit's midpoint—we conduct another whole-group assessment to determine next steps. See Figure 2.8.

Figure 2.8 Needs Assessment Midway Through the Unit

Whole Group Assessment and Sorting Sheet

Unit: Personal Narrative   Date: 8/29/13

Writing Quality: Explode Moment — Kids who need help with this:	Student Mentor Text:	Writing Quality: Leads/Endings — Kids who need help with this:	Student Mentor Text:
Morgan Maddie Jaden Zoe Isabelle Tyler Luke Connor Brynne Marie Kathryn Matthew MOST	Loan Ashley Hailey Kelly Jo Nicholas	Jax Zoe Isabelle Henry Luke Kathryn) Most Brynne Trevor Matthew Chase Maddie Loan	Brandon Ashley Kelly Jo
Writing Quality: Focus/Angling — Kids who need help with this:	Student Mentor Text:	Writing Quality: Ending Punctuation — Kids who need help with this:	Student Mentor Text:
ALL	Pre-teach to Ashley	Morgan Connor Jaden (and) Trevor Isabelle Chase Brynne (Then) Nicole Matthew Maddie MOST	Henry Abby
Writing Quality: Quotation Marks — Kids who need help with this: Speaker tags	Student Mentor Text:	Writing Quality: Volume — Kids who need help with this:	Student Mentor Text:
Jax Trevor Isabelle Nicole Maddie Connor Zoe Kathryn		All Students! Change to paper w/more lines & discuss expectations with kids.	

Writing Goals/Minilessons based on this data:

1. Explode the Moment
2. Leads/Endings (Craft/Connect)
3. Focus/Angling
4. Ending punct./Dialogue

May be photocopied for classroom use. © 2015 by Lisa Eickholdt from *Learning from Classmates: Using Students' Writing as Mentor Texts*. Portsmouth, NH: Heinemann.

While most students are focusing their writing, some are still writing sparsely (students sometimes think writing about a small moment means making their writing shorter). In the primary grades, one way to prompt students to write longer stories is to use paper with more lines, which we do. The students are also giving every part of their story—beginning, middle, and end—equal attention. They don't understand that the most important moments in a story should be richly detailed. Deb and I decide to teach them an elaboration strategy called *exploding the moment* (Lane 1999, 97), in which writers slow down the most important moment or moments by adding lots of detail. The students also need help crafting interesting beginnings and satisfying endings. Based on this midpoint assessment, we create the lesson plan shown in Figure 2.9.

Evaluating Our Teaching

Though the terms *assessment* and *evaluation* are often used interchangeably, they are not identical. Assessment is the ongoing collection of data to inform our teaching. Evaluation is a conclusion about an end product that results in a score or grade (Rhodes and Shanklin 1993). As teachers we are required to both assess and evaluate our students. We can use the form in Figure 2.10 to guide our evaluations of our students' final published pieces, assess our teaching, and choose a couple of pieces of student writing to copy and retain as mentor texts.

Figure 2.9 Lesson Plan Addressing Midpoint Writing Goals

Lesson Planning Sheet

Unit: Personal Narrative 2nd grade Dates: 8/29 – 9/2

Writing Goals: Elaborate most important part, leads/endings
Focus/angling piece

Writing Goal/Quality	Teaching Methods/Lessons
Leads – answer – who? what? where? - Describe setting - Thinking	Children's Literature: Owl Moon by Yolen (setting) My writing – thinking
Endings – wrap things up & connect to lead. - Thinking	- Owl Moon - My writing
Elaborate most imp. part/ explode the moment	Student Mentor Text: - Ashley - Nicholas
Explode the Moment	Children's Literature: Owl Moon (when they finally see the owl).
Focus around an idea/ angle your writing	Student Mentor Text: Ashley

May be photocopied for classroom use. © 2015 by Lisa Eickholdt from *Learning from Classmates: Using Students' Writing as Mentor Texts*. Portsmouth, NH: Heinemann.

Date: _____   Unit of Study: _____

Figure 2.10 End-of-Unit Reflection Guide

What changes do I need to make to improve my instruction the next time I teach my students and the next time I teach this study?

[Students' writing is a direct reflection of the teaching they have received. Paying attention to the patterns in your students' work will alert you to changes you need to make to improve your instruction. You can immediately use things you notice during this unit's postassessment that relate generally to the writing process to create instructional goals in your next unit of study. For the future, you can keep in mind things that are specific to the genre or the unit focused on.]

What student mentor text should I keep to use in future studies?

[Good examples of student writing should be copied and placed in a binder to use as models in lessons and conferences in later units of study and in future years.]

Our end-of-unit reflection for the second-grade narrative writing unit, shown in Figure 2.11, reveals what Deb and I need to work on in our teaching. Though our next unit of study will be on informational writing, we can address specificity and "show, not tell" in any genre. We didn't teach specificity at all in this unit (and it shows), but we did work on showing, not telling. However, the kids' writing demonstrates more work needs to be done. The other qualities on our list—more meaningful dialogue, quotation marks and speaker tags, and sensory language—are more genre specific. We'll tuck this information away and keep it in mind the next time we teach a narrative study.

Figure 2.11 End-of-Unit Reflection Guide

End of Unit Reflection Guide

Date: **9/20**   Unit of Study: Personal Narrative
                                       Second grade

What changes do I need to make to improve my instruction the next time I teach these kids and the next time I teach this study?

More instruction on how to:

- Use dialogue meaningfully
- Use quotation marks and speaker tags.
- Specificity with word choice.
- Include more sensory language.
- Show - not tell.

What student mentor text should I keep to use in future studies?

Zoe - Pumpkin Patch Picking

Nicholas - Grandpa's Visit

Things to keep in mind

Immersion

* Expose students to the genre: Immerse students before they write by reading lots of great mentor texts. This activity will give them a sense of the genre.

* Chart it: Work with students to highlight the key features of a genre. Post these on a class anchor chart.

* Choose wisely: Choose mentor texts that are filled with great craft so you can return to these same texts over and over again for different teaching points.

* Give a copy: Provide students with a copy of the mentor text to store in their writing folders. They can then return to the text over and over again as they are writing.

* Name it: Be sure to name the writing technique for students. Remember, naming something makes it repeatable.

* Don't assume compliance: Just because you tell students to do something, don't assume they will. Instead, help students understand why they should use a certain writing technique. Explain why it's effective. Show students how it will help them as writers or how it improves their writing.

Assessment

* Begin at the beginning: Assess your group of students before a unit of study so you can plan lessons that are responsive to their needs.

* Determine what you value: Decide what writing traits you value most. Then, search for these in your students' work.

* Choose a few teaching points: Decide what your students need to learn. Choose several goals for your group and plan lessons that support these goals.

* Search for student mentor texts: As you search for needs, search for possible mentor texts. Though many of your kids need help with a certain writing technique, there will be a few students who don't. Use these students' writing as mentor texts in your lessons.

* Repeat the process: Reassess your group midway through a unit to determine how best to meet students' current needs. Set new goals and create new lessons to support these needs.

* Reflect: Analyze your groups' writing after a study. Their writing is a mirror of your teaching. Reflect on how you can improve as a teacher.

Conferences

Keeping an Eye on Identifying Powerful Elements in Student Writing

> Conferring with children is an art. It's an active process wherein we sit side by side with children, put ourselves in the moment, listen carefully, and reflect in ways that encourage and nudge them forward as learners.
>
> —*Debbie Miller*

A writing workshop has three basic components: the lesson; independent writing while the teacher confers with individuals; and sharing. What sets workshop teaching apart from other types of instruction is conferring: Workshop pedagogy is sometimes referred to as the conference approach to teaching. When we confer with students every day, we have the opportunity to meet every child's needs and teach them something new. As Johnston (2004) points out, teaching is more meaningful when we focus on what students are attempting to do—the cutting edge of their learning. Lucy Calkins (2003) suggests that we approach a conference thinking, "What has the child done—or gestured toward doing—that represents the outer edge of the child's development and therefore would be wise for me to extol?" (75). Keeping this in mind helps ensure that every conference positively impacts the writer.

THE CONFERENCE STRUCTURE: A QUICK REVIEW

Calkins (1994) states, "These conferences are at the heart of our teaching" (189). Conferring may be the heart of writing workshop, but for many writing teachers it is the hardest part. One reason is because knowing exactly what to say to each student can be difficult. Many of us find it helps to follow a predictable structure: research, decide, teach, and link (Calkins 1994; Anderson 2000).

Research

At their core, writing conferences are conversations. Though the goal is to teach the student how to become a better writer, the form this teaching takes is a discussion between two individuals. Typically I sit beside the student so I can look her in the eye, as opposed to standing above her (an authoritative stance that doesn't encourage open communication). As in all conversations, the participants have roles to play (Anderson 2000). I generally initiate the conversation, then quickly turn the conversation over to the child so I can begin my research.

I begin every conference with a predictable question, such as "How's it going?" (Anderson 2000) or "What are your plans for this piece?" My hope is that later on as they write, my students will pause and ask themselves this same important question. In the end, it doesn't really matter what question I ask, as long as it gets students to talk about their writing. As the student talks, I listen closely and read his writing.

Decide (and Compliment)

As I assess each writer, I make two important instructional decisions: what to compliment and what to teach (Calkins 2003). Although a compliment is a form of encouragement, naming the reason for it turns this praise into a teachable moment. Katherine Bomer (2010) proposes that teachers begin every conference by noticing what the student is doing (or attempting to do), praising her for it, and then naming it.

> I believe this naming portion of the writing conference is not a throwaway moment, not empty praise, or a pat on the head for being a good girl or boy, but in fact the key to teaching students something they may not have consciously realized they are doing so they can build on it and do it again. (9)

Complimenting and naming make students aware of what they are unknowingly doing, enabling them to repeat the process in the future.

Recently, I took my family snow skiing for the first time. Because I hadn't skied in years and my husband and son were both new skiers, I signed us up for a beginner lesson. During this session, my son, Jack, accidently began skiing down the small slope on which we were working. I watched him quickly pick up speed and was sure he'd fall. Instead, he naturally began spreading the backs of his skis apart. As the instructor praised him and encouraged him to continue this maneuver, Jack slowed to a stop. She continued to make a big deal of this, applauding him for "snowplowing." Her compliment, quickly followed by a label, helped Jack and the rest understand one method skiers use to slow themselves down and stop. The rest of the day found us snowplowing down the slopes (in my case, the bunny hill!).

Teach

In making my teaching decision, I contemplate both the child's intentions as well as his needs. In essence, it's a multiple-choice question with several answers to choose from: (a) reteach a strategy recently taught in the lesson; (b) teach a new strategy; or (c) address a specific issue or need. Whatever choice I make, it is always my goal to teach the writer one new thing that will help him the most at this time and in the future. This doesn't mean I don't notice many other things I need to teach him; however, I choose just one for this moment. Keeping in mind that I will have many opportunities over the year to work with a student counteracts my tendency to try to teach too many things at once, which can make the writer feel my job is to correct all his mistakes rather than to help him become a better writer. My teaching decisions must be based on how to best help the writer, not improve the writing (Calkins 2003).

After I decide what I will teach, my instruction takes one of three forms: using a mentor text as a model, demonstrating the strategy, or guiding the child through the process step by step. Often I employ a mixture of all three. Then, I leave the student with a concrete plan for doing this new work and move on only after I get him started. Often, I'll also ask him to show me his work when he finishes, or I'll stop back later to check in.

Link

To conclude the conference, I reiterate the teaching point and link it with the student's ongoing work. I repeat the name of the strategy and mention how this writing concept can help her in her current and future work. "Every time you're writing and you're trying to [name of strategy] you can always [description of strategy]." The work done during a conference isn't a one-time fix but can be used each and every time a student writes.

IDENTIFYING STUDENT WRITING TO USE AS A MENTOR TEXT

When I confer, my mind is on two things: the individual student and the whole group. As I talk with a student about how to grow as a writer, I'm also aware of what I need to teach the rest of my students. I ask myself, "What is this child doing that I can use in my teaching in some way?" During the compliment or teaching portion of the conference, I may notice the student has implemented (or attempted to implement) something taught in a recent lesson. Or he may implement the strategy we focus on in the conference in a particularly effective way. If the rest of the students could benefit from having more instruction on this concept, I invite him to help me teach an upcoming lesson.

Any kind of work I do with an individual student can support group learning. In a conference, I'm either reteaching a concept taught in a recent lesson, teaching something new, or helping the student with a specific problem. Each type of instruction can produce a student mentor text.

Finding Student Mentor Texts in Reteaching Conferences

Conferences in which I reteach concepts or strategies I've introduced in recent lessons often produce work I can feature in an upcoming lesson. Here's an example. Early in the year I taught a second-grade classroom a lesson on how to bring characters to life by making them move and talk (Hartman and Mooney 2013; Martinelli and Mraz 2012). I had the following conference with Zoe immediately afterward:

> **Me:** Hey, Zoe! What are you working on?
>
> **Zoe:** I'm writing a story about going to the pumpkin patch.
>
> **Me:** That sounds like fun. How's it going?
>
> **Zoe:** Good.
>
> **Me:** Can you read me what you have so far?
>
> **Zoe:** Sure. [*Zoe reads her piece; see Figure 3.1.*]

Figure 3.1 Zoe's Preconference Writing

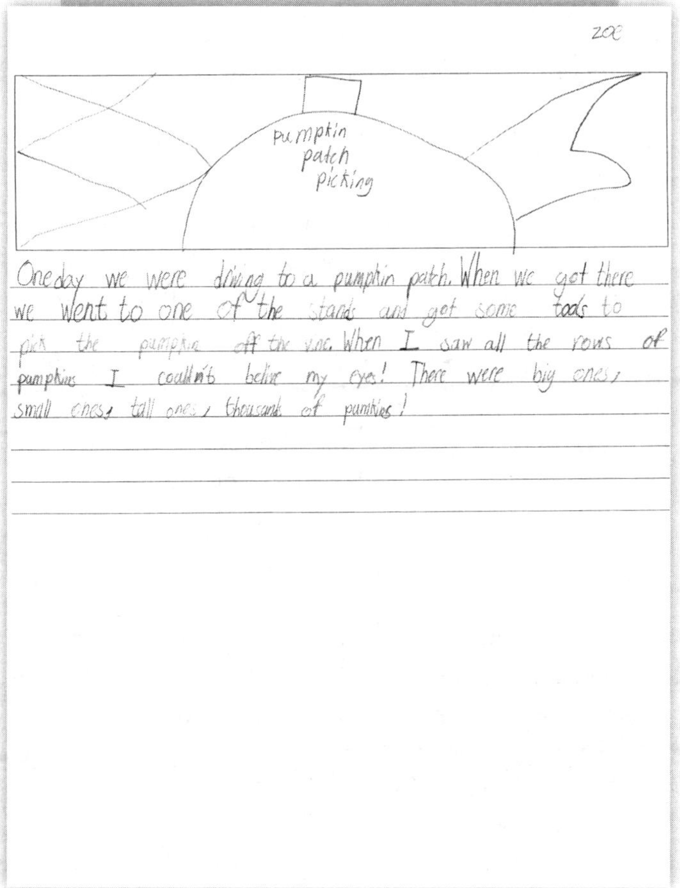

Zoe

pumpkin
patch
picking

One day we were driving to a pumpkin patch. When we get there we went to one of the stands and got some tools to pick the pumpkin off the vine. When I saw all the rows of pumpkins I couldn't belive my eyes! There were big ones, small ones, tall ones, thousands of pumkins!

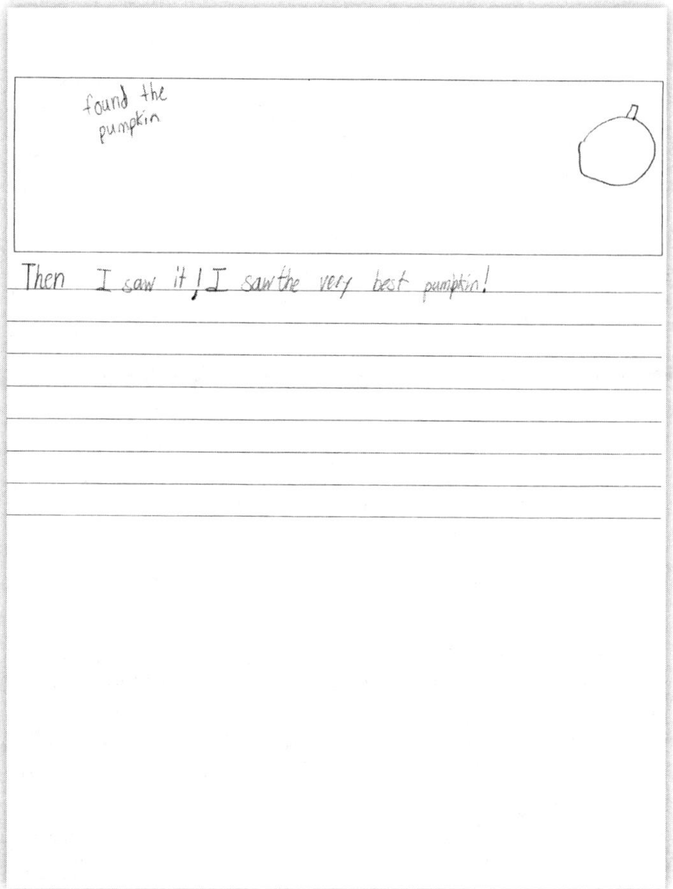

found the
pumpkin

Then I saw it! I saw the very best pumpkin!

cut
the
pumpkin

Me: Great start to your story, Zoe! I really like a couple of things about this piece. I noticed you jotted down a few words at the top of each page to help you remember your ideas. We've been talking about how writers always plan before they write, and the notes you made are one way to do that. You'll always want to make sure you take time to plan before you write. The other thing I liked was the part when you saw the pumpkins. I love how you used a little list to describe them! You wrote, "When I saw all the pumpkins I couldn't believe my eyes! There were big ones, tall ones, small ones, thousands of pumpkins!" That is a beautiful description. I can really picture it. Using a repeating list like that makes it sound like a published piece of writing. It reminds me of the book *Millions of Cats*. The writer says the same kind of thing when she sees a lot of cats: "There were hundreds of cats, thousands of cats, millions and billions and trillions of cats!" Have you read that book? Is that maybe where you got the idea for that part?

Zoe [*shaking her head*]: No, I just thought that would sound good.

Me: Well, you were right about that. I love that little list. It sounds like something I would read in a book. Good work! [*Zoe smiles.*] So what are you going to do now? What are your plans for the rest of this piece?

Zoe: I'm going to try and do what Nicholas did in his story.

Me: Oh, so you're going to try to bring your characters alive by having them talk and move. Can you show me where?

Zoe: Sure. Right here [*points to the second page*]. After I find the pumpkin I want, I'm going to yell, "I want that one!" Then I'm going to run over and hug it!

Me: Great! You're doing what Nicholas did in his piece! I like how you're bringing your characters to life by making them talk and move. That always makes a story more interesting. That's really going to add a lot to that part. Good job. Are you going to try that anywhere else in the piece?

Zoe [*looking through her piece*]: No. I just thought it would be good to do that there.

Zoe wisely realizes that she needs to elaborate her story but intends to do so in only one part of her piece. This response is typical. Young writers generally attempt a new writing technique very sparingly, and I need to teach them that writers use the same techniques over and over. Many other students in the class will respond the way Zoe did and require the same instruction.

Me: Okay, but one thing you'll want to remember is that when writers learn how to use a writing technique, they don't use it in just one part of their book; they use it throughout the book. Making your people move and talk is something you can do on every page, not just on one.

Zoe: Oh.

Me: Let's look at how Nicholas did that throughout his piece, on almost every page. [*I bring out Nicholas's story, Figure 3.2, and Zoe and I read through it.*]

Figure 3.2 Nicholas's Story, "Grandpa's Visit"

Page 1

Grampa's Visit

One day me & my little brother were wating for my grama & grapa to come to my house. They live in Iowa. I sat down on the couch for an hour. I said "when are they going to get here?" "Soon" my mom said. I hadent seen them for a long time.

Page 2

BOOM! SMASH BANG SHATER! CRASH!

I sat for ONE MORE HOUR!!! after that I couldent take it! My body started to sqwrme, my legs kicked, my head tilt. I was going to exploed! I WAS FERES!!!

Page 3

when I calmered down I went down stairs to play my video games & to wait. I played for a little bit. Finally my mom yelled "There here! there here!" It was so exsiting! I ran up stairs. I asked "where, where?" My heart was beating so hard. I yelled "Yay!" I ran to the door.

Page 4

My grandpa was wating there. Then I remembred he was go to tickle us. He opend the door. His fingers ran up & down my stomck. I kicked at him. I laughed yelling "stop stop!" I ran a way.

Page 5

stop!!!

It was a long week because of all the ticling... but I kinda liked it!

See how Nicholas did that? Remember, Nicholas said he thought back to the time and tried to remember exactly what he was doing and what he probably said, and then he wrote it down. Let's go back to the first page of your story and try those things now. Think back to that time, play the movie in your mind, and think about what you were doing, particularly what your body might have been doing and what you might have been saying when you saw all those pumpkins.

Zoe: Well—when I saw all the pumpkins—I ran over to them really fast.

Me: Okay, good. Then what?

Zoe: I ran ahead of my mom and dad. And my dad yelled for me to come back.

Me: Okay. Then what happened?

Zoe: Then I saw all those pumpkins, and I couldn't believe it. I was so excited that I was going to get to cut one for the first time.

Me: What did you say?

Zoe: I think I told my dad that I was excited.

Me: Great! Do you see how you played the movie of that moment in your mind and focused on how you were moving and what you were saying? Now you can go back and add those things.

Zoe: Yeah.

Me: You can do the same thing on this last page. Think back to that time and how you were moving and what you were saying. Okay?

Zoe: Okay.

Me: Zoe, I love what you're planning to do in this piece. Every time you write, remember you can use a strategy over and over throughout your whole story, not just in one part. Bringing your characters to life by making them move and talk is something you will want to do in every story you write from now on. Would you please help me teach the others how to do this in tomorrow's lesson? I want you to show everyone how you used that strategy not just in one place but throughout your whole piece.

Zoe: You mean sit up there? [*She points to the chairs at the front of our meeting area.*]

Me: Yes, sit up there, and help me teach.

Zoe [*smiling*]: Yay!

Zoe was doing two things I felt the other students needed help with—using a fabulous elaboration technique and applying that technique across her piece. Her revised piece is shown in Figure 3.3.

Figure 3.3 Zoe's Piece After Our Conference
on Bringing Characters to Life

One day we were driving to a pumpkin patch. When we got there we went to one of the stands and got some tools to plek the pumpkins off the vine. When I saw all the rows of pumpkins I couldn't beleve my eyes! Ther were big ones, small ones, tall ones, thousands of pumpkins. I started runing fast like we were playing tag or having a race. "Stop Zoe! Come back!" My dad said. Then I stoped. I whispeed, "I nver seen this many pumpkins!" "This will be the frist time we cut the pumpkin off the vine." I said.

Then I saw it! I saw the very best pumpkin. "I want that one" I yelled. I ran over as fast as a cheta is trying to get his pray be for the otle cheeta takes it. When I got there I hugged it. Then my parents came over. "Are you sher you want this pumpkin?" My dad said cathing his breath. "YES!" I replied quikly.

Then f'inaly after he caught his breath he gave me the tools. And then I strated to clip th vine & I felt scard. "Need some help?" My dad asked. "Yes I guse so." I said softly. I holded the tools and my dad holded my hands. I closed one eye and turned my head... then right after I turned my heal my hands wiggled and giggled and strated to bounce... when I opened my exes... I did it, and I didn't even feel it! "Jack-o-latern here I come!" I started to chip to the car like I was little red riding going to her granmas house happy as can be. When I got home I started planning my Jack-o-latern.

Finding Student Mentor Texts in "Teaching Something New" Conferences

My workshop teaching is based on individualized instruction, and some students are ready to tackle new writing techniques sooner than others. I not only expect but hope this will happen. To successfully differentiate instruction and support all learners, I need an in-depth understanding of writing. According to Ray (2006):

> Conferring, the one-to-one teaching of individual writers in a workshop, is greatly enhanced as the teacher's knowledge base grows (Anderson 2000). Quite simply, the more teachers know, the better they confer and the more they have to offer in terms of differentiated instruction. (29)

An in-depth knowledge of various writing strategies, techniques, and genres gives me a variety of teaching points to draw on as I confer with students at all levels. I use three main ways to acquire the knowledge I need. First, I write myself. There is no substitute for doing the kind of writing I am asking my students to do. I can then speak from experience in a conference and say, "When I am having trouble doing [strategy], I have found it helpful to [explanation]." Second, I read the genres I am teaching. Former US Poet Laureate Ted Kooser suggests that before writing one poem, one must first read a hundred. Observing what the best children's authors are doing in their writing gives me a range of teaching points to draw from in my work with kids. Third, I read professional books, study the work of other writing teachers, and discover teaching approaches that may be appropriate for my students. Knowing a range of teaching possibilities is invaluable.

Teaching something new in a conference is an impetus to moving my teaching along. When conferring with a student who is ready to learn a new technique, I consider whether the work is something the rest of the class is ready to learn as well. And because every writing concept entails instruction from simple to complex, I can also use my conferences to help students refine a particular skill or strategy.

Here's an example of a conference in which I teach something new. It's the end of the school year in a kindergarten class, and I've just begun a how-to unit. The kids love this kind of writing and are churning out procedural texts on how to do a variety of things: throw a baseball, make a sandwich, brush your teeth. However, many of the students, including Owen, struggle with including enough details in each step of the process.

Me: Hi, Owen! What are you working on today?

Owen: I'm trying to teach people how to shoot a basketball.

Me: Do you like to play basketball?

Owen: Yeah.

Me: Are you on a team or do you just play at home?

Owen: I just play at home with my friends.

Me: That sounds like fun. Can you read your piece to me?

Owen: Sure. [*He reads the piece shown in Figure 3.4.*]

Me: Owen, I really like the tip you wrote on the first page. Can you explain it to me though? I'm not sure what it means.

Figure 3.4 Owen's Preconference Piece on Shooting a Basketball

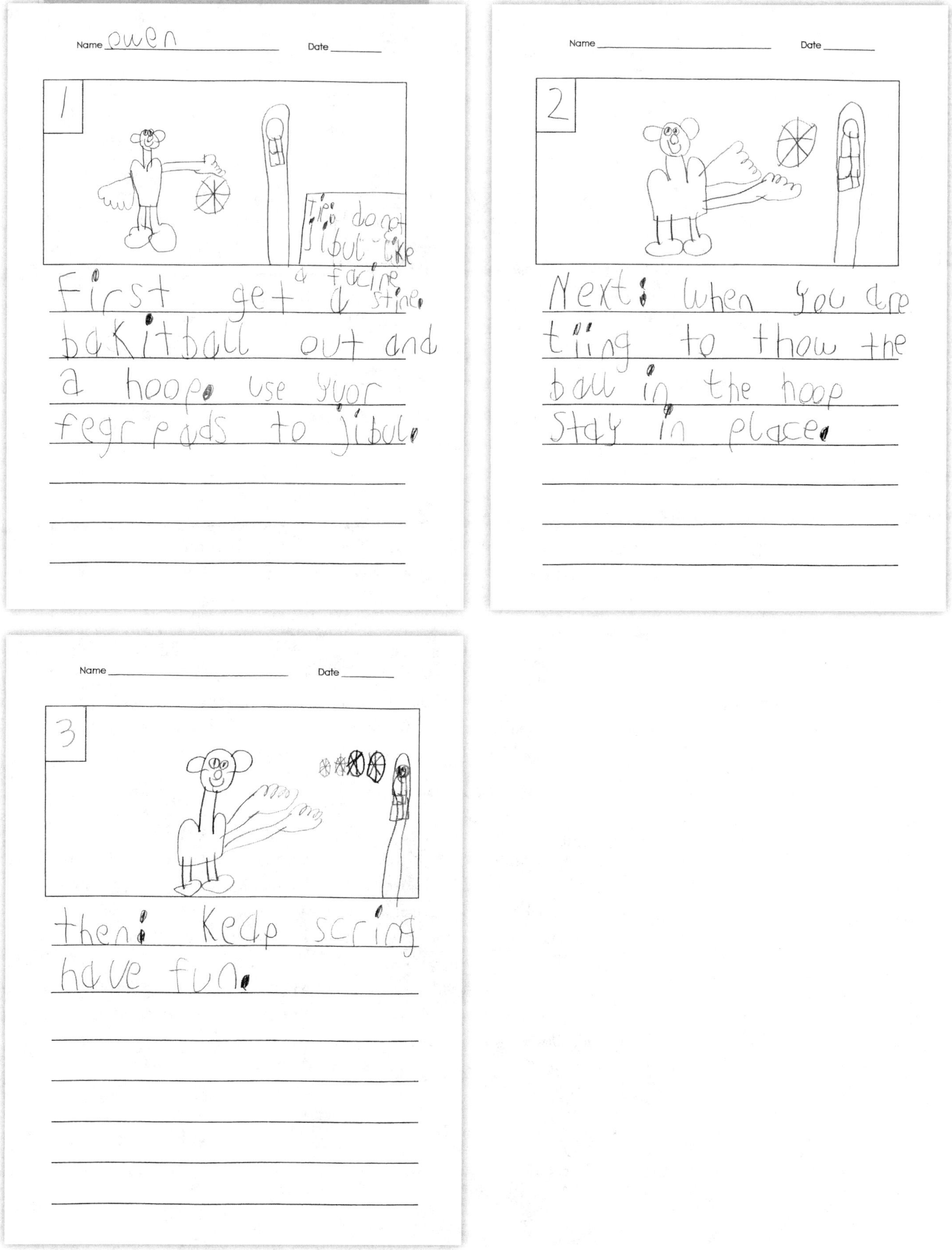
Name owen
Date
1
Tip: do not jibul like a facine stine.
First get a bakitball out and a hoop. use yuor fegr pads to jibul.
Name
Date
2
Next: when you are tiing to thow the ball in the hoop Stay in place.
Name
Date
3
then: Keap scring have fun.

Owen: It says, don't dribble like a Frankenstein. Because you're supposed to use your finger pads to dribble. Not with your hand flat like this [*holding his hand out flat and pretending to dribble*]. I wrote that right there [*pointing to first page*].

Me: Oh, so when you're dribbling you're supposed to use the pads of your fingers and not the flat part of your hand. I didn't know that. That's a really good tip! Tips are supposed to teach your reader something important, and that's exactly what yours did. Good job! Every time I dribble a basketball now, I will be trying not to dribble like a Frankenstein! [*Owen smiles.*] What are your plans for this piece now? What are you going to do next?

Owen: I'm going to make a cover and staple it together.

Me: Oh, you're done with it?

Owen: Yeah.

Although Owen feels this piece is done and ready to finish, I have other plans. It is clear he needs to revise and add more details to each step. As he acted out for me how not to dribble like a Frankenstein, I decided to teach Owen something totally new. I often teach students to add precise actions to their stories by thinking about what their legs, hands, or eyes are doing at key moments (Anderson 2009). This strategy also works well in procedural texts, particularly those in which the writer is explaining how to do something sports-related. Others in the class can benefit from learning this strategy as well.

Me: Before you put a cover on this book and finish it, I'd like to teach you something. Your acting out how to dribble the basketball gave me an idea. Do you remember when we were writing about small moments, and we learned that writers add specific actions to their pieces by describing exactly what their hands, legs, and eyes are doing?

Owen: Yeah.

Me: Well, I think if you did that in this piece, it would make it easier for people to understand. That's what you want when you write a how-to book. You want every step to have enough details to teach someone how to do exactly what you're describing. You started doing that on this first page, when you explained exactly what to do with your hands. You wrote, "Use your finger pads to dribble." You taught me what to do with my hands. Now let's see if you can tell people exactly what to do with their legs and eyes. You might want to stand up and act out exactly what you need to do with your body to help you do this. [*Owen acts out dribbling the ball, pretending the garbage can is a basket.*] What are you doing with your legs?

Owen: Walking.

Me: Be more specific.

Owen: I'm moving my feet to the basket.

Me: Good. What about your eyes. What are they doing?

Owen: Umm, I'm looking at the ball.

Me: So we could add that part to this page. Move your feet to the basket. Keep your eyes on the ball. That makes this step so much clearer! Quick, come write that down. [*Owen sits down and writes.*] Let's see if we can do the same kind of work on the next page.

Owen: Okay.

Me: On this page you're trying to explain how to shoot the ball. You wrote, "Next, when you are dribbling the ball, stay in place." Why don't you get up and act it out again? What part of your body are you describing when you say that?

Owen: Your legs. You have to stop when you go to shoot.

Me: So now what? [*Owen gets up and mimics reaching up his arms and throwing the ball in the basket, verbalizing what his arms and eyes are doing. He quickly jots it down and reads his revised page.*] Wow! That's a lot better! What do you think?

Owen: Yeah, it's way better!

Me: Great! Every time you write a how-to book, you'll want to use lots of details to explain exactly how to do each step. One way to include more details is to tell what your arms, legs, and eyes are doing in each step. Acting it out will help you add those details. I'm going to confer with Sammy now, but you might want to look at your last page and see if you can add more there too. I would love it if you helped me teach this strategy to the other kids. Will you help me teach the lesson tomorrow?

Owen: You mean be famous?

Me: Yes, be famous.

Owen: Yes! [*Owen's piece as he revised it after our conference is shown in Figure 3.5.*]

Finding Student Mentor Texts in Troubleshooting Conferences

Every child isn't ready to tackle current and upcoming writing strategies and techniques. Meeting students where they are sometimes means clearing up confusions or troubleshooting in a conference. If the needs of one student are representative of many of my students, I take a step back and clear up the confusion for the rest of the group.

The most common type of troubleshooting conference relates to the writing process. In every unit of study, I teach genre-specific methods to help students generate ideas, plan, revise, and edit. When the unit is under way, I focus more on crafting techniques to help improve content. Conferences in which I reteach a process strategy remind me that I need to revisit process strategies throughout a unit.

I'll give an example. I'm circulating in a fifth-grade classroom while the students are writing when my eye is drawn to John. During the last few minutes he's gotten

Figure 3.5 Owen's Piece After Our Conference on Adding Precise Actions

Name OWEN _____   Date _____

1

First get a bakitball out and a hoop. use ruer fegr pads to jidul. Move your feet to the bakit. kdep your des on the ball

Name _____   Date _____

2

Next: when you are tiing to thow the ball in the hoop stay in place. strch your arms up and thow the ball. kdep your bes on the bakit

Name _____   Date _____

3

then grab the ball when it comes down. keap scring. have fun up to sharpen his pencil, gaze around the room, and talk to other students. Then he asks if he can go to the bathroom. John usually doesn't usually avoid writing like this, so I investigate.

Me: John. How's it going today?

John: Umm, not good.

Me: Oh, I'm sorry. Why?

John: I don't know what to write about!

Me: I see. That's frustrating. I hate when that happens.

John: Yeah, it's like there are no stories left!

Me: Really? Well, we've talked a lot about having writing territories to work from [Atwell 2007]. Have you figured out some of your writing territories?

John: Yeah. I like to write about football, traveling, school, and my dog. [*He shows me the list of writing territories in Figure 3.6.*]

Figure 3.6 John's List of Writing Territories

Me: Have you done some writing on any of these topics?

John: Yeah. I wrote a couple of stories about my dog, Daisy.

Lisa: Can you show me?

John: Sure. Here is one where I wrote about when we got Daisy. We got her from a rescue place. She came running out and just started licking me and jumping on me. [*Flips through more pages in his notebook.*] Here is a story about how she got up underneath my mattress one time and was climbing around under there. My mom couldn't believe it! She chewed a hole in that black material and climbed up inside it.

Me: Daisy sounds like quite a dog! Is she a little bit crazy?

John: Yeah. My mom calls her Crazy Daisy!

Me: That's funny! So you've written two entries about Daisy so far.

John: Yeah.

Lisa: Do you have any others?

John: No.

My teaching decision here is easy. John has told me he's having trouble coming up with an idea to write about; I need to help him. Although he has listed some topics or territories he likes to write about, he hasn't dug deeply into those topics. (Young writers often believe one or two entries cover all they have to say about something.) When I modeled this writing strategy for the class, I showed how one territory could be used to generate many ideas, so I need to clear up John's misconception. Also, I've observed other kids in the class taking longer and longer to begin writing, so I suspect many other students are confused about fully exploring their writing territories. I can teach John how to generate more ideas from a writing territory and use this experience in a future lesson.

Me: Well, you've done some great work figuring out your writing territories—topics that writers write about over and over again. I also like how you have already written a couple of entries about one territory, your dog, Daisy. That's all good work! But can I teach you something today?

John: Sure.

Me: When we talked about writing territories, we learned that writers don't write just one or two stories on these topics. They're called territories because they encompass lots of little stories. You've written a couple of stories about Daisy, but my hunch is you have a lot more left to tell. That's like me and my son, Jack: I don't have just one or two stories about him; I have lots and lots—hundreds, in fact. To help me think of stories I could write about Jack, I could make a little list. Jack is my big topic, and all the stories I have about him are subtopics, starting with the phrase, "The time . . . ." Let me show you how that looks. [*I make a list in my notebook of stories about my son, briefly discussing each one.*] Now it's your turn. Let's try making a list of Daisy stories. Tell me some of the times you remember with her.

John: I remember the time she jumped up on our kitchen table before dinner and started lapping up all the sour cream my mom put out for the baked potatoes.

Me: Yuck! She is crazy! That would make a great story. What else?

John: Once she jumped out the car window, and I had to chase her all the way down the street before I caught her.

Me: Great! Go to a clean page in your notebook, and start jotting down these ideas. Start by putting Daisy at the top. Then, underneath, list all the stories you can remember about her. It will help if you start each item in your list with, *The time* . . . . Every time you're stuck and don't know what to write about, go back to one of your writing territories, and list all the little stories you can think about for that bigger topic.

John: Got it! [*John's list is shown in Figure 3.7.*]

Me: John, can you please help me teach this to everyone in tomorrow's lesson? I think lots of other kids are also confused.

John: Sure!

Figure 3.7 John's List of Possible Daisy Stories After Our Conference

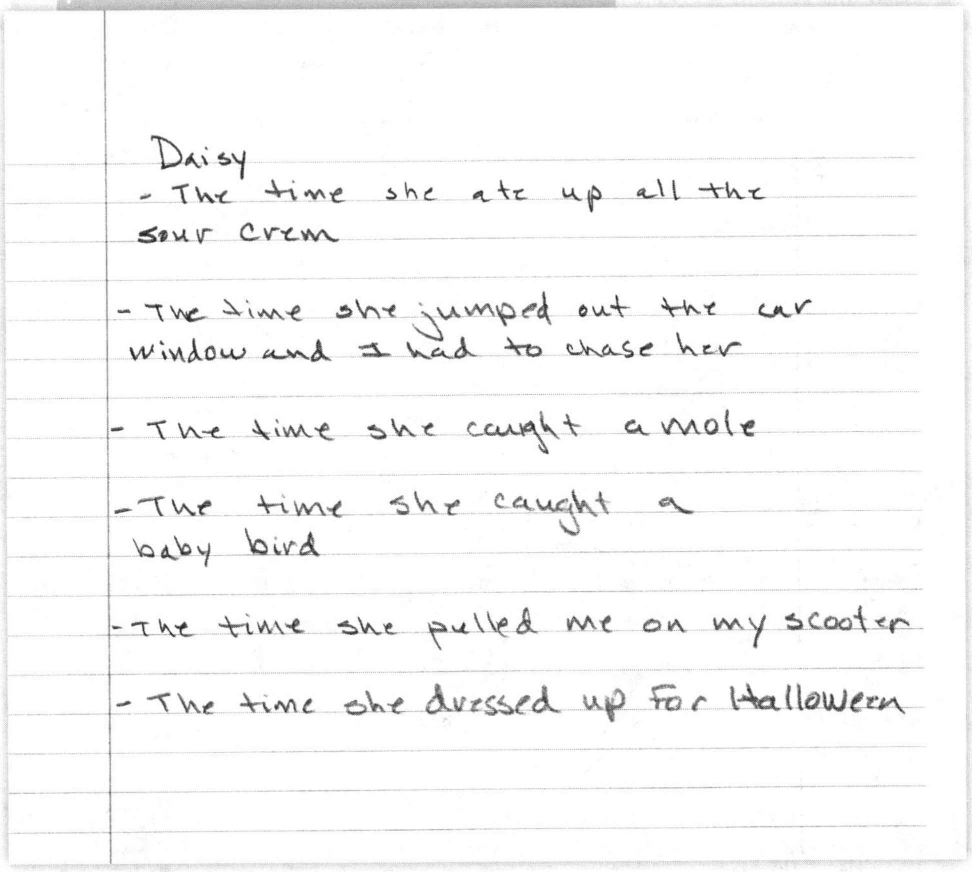

Daisy
- The time she ate up all the sour crem
- The time she jumped out the car window and I had to chase her
- The time she caught a mole
- The time she caught a baby bird
- The time she pulled me on my scooter
- The time she dressed up For Halloween

KEEPING CONFERENCE RECORDS

Keeping records is an integral part of conferring. Anecdotal notes help me tailor my instruction to meet the needs of each child and help me identify student mentor texts. However, these notes can't be helpful if they're not used, and they won't be used if they're not simple and accessible. Lots of simple ways to keep anecdotal records are available: computer labels, index cards, tabbed notebooks, assessment apps, customized forms (see the examples in Figures 3.8 and 3.9). I use two forms, a class checklist and anecdotal records sheets, which I store in a three-ring binder.

Figure 3.8 A Kindergarten Teacher's Anecdotal Records

★ =Mentor Text

Student: Alec Date: 8/27 Title of piece: ★I see a ___ Observations: -Pattern book -Needs help with illustrating- 　　　　　　　background Teaching Point: ★Use a similar sentence pattern on every page.	Student: Justin Date: 8/27 Title of piece: Trucks Observations: -Already labeling -Already stretching words. Teaching Point: -Use sentences to create a pattern book.
Student: Mary Date: 8/27 Title of piece: Fishing Story Observations: -Noticing speech "Him gets my pole!" Worked-"He gets my..." Teaching Point: -Got out ABC strip-practiced stretching word out & writing letters	Student: Savannah Date: 8/27 Title of piece: The Beach Observations: Likes to draw, but not writing words. Doesn't seem to Teaching Point: know sounds. -Add details to pictures. (background, clothes, hair, etc.)
Student: John Date: 8/28 Title of piece: ★Batman Observations: Very excited to write about Batman! Add Robin. Teaching Point: ★Use speech bubbles to make people talk.	Student: Ashley Date: 8/28 Title of piece: My Birthday Observations: Only draws one single thing in middle of page. Teaching Point: No labels Fill up pages with drawings! Add background.
Student: Brandon Date: 8/28 Title of piece: ★Swimming Observations: Telling a story across pages. Great pictures! Teaching Point: ★Show how characters are feeling in pictures (smile/ frown etc.)	Student: Date: Title of piece: Observations: Teaching Point:
Student: Date: Title of piece: Observations: Teaching Point:	Student: Date: Title of piece: Observations: Teaching Point:

Figure 3.9 A Fourth-Grade Teacher's Anecdotal Records

Mrs. Nannis
Writing Workshop

Week of: 4/4 - 4/8

☑ =Observation
TP=Teaching Point
★=Mentor Text

Norah	Grace	Mackenzie	Adrian	Emma
★ Great text features (timeline) T.P. - Check on accuracy of facts.				
Mallory	Jack	John	Beth	James
		✓Good overall Structure! T.P. Use transitions to help w/ elaboration	T.P. Organize notes before drafting.	
Chandler	Jake	Brandon	Parker	Natalie
		✓ Very detailed narr. section. T.P. - Use specific words to paint pict.		T.P. - Try out various text Structures before choosing one.
Joshua	Matt	Sam	Tracy	Tricia
		★ Great parallel list! T.P. - All supp. details must support main idea		
Holly	Caleb	Hannah	Josh	Mandi
T.P. Define vocabulary (taught three ways).				

Class Checklist

The class checklist (see Figures 3.10 and 3.11) helps me keep track of the date conferences occur. I type in each student's name and make several copies. Then, every time I confer with a student, I jot down the date of the conference. A regular quick glance at this list ensures I am meeting with every child as often as possible.

Figure 3.10 Blank Class Checklist

STUDENT	DATE	DATE	DATE	DATE

Anecdotal Record Sheet

I record each important element of a conference—teaching point, other possible goals, when the student's writing was used as a mentor text—on an anecdotal record sheet (see Figures 3.12 and 3.13). At the beginning of the year, I make six or so copies of the form for each child and place them in a binder with tabbed sections. (Some teachers assign students numbers so they don't need to change the names on the tabs each year.)

Date/Title

In this box I enter the date of the conference (to cross-reference the class checklist) and the title of the student's piece. The title may initially seem unnecessary, but it's important because it jars my memory of these conversations. If I fill out only the other

Figure 3.11 A Completed Class Checklist

Student	Date	Date	Date	Date
Will	9/13	9/21		
Harry	9/15	9/22		
Alan	9/16	9/23	9/27	
Valerie	9/16	9/22		
Connor	9/13	9/20		
Natalie	9/16	9/29		
Ken	9/17	9/29		
Jaden	9/13	9/20		
Brook	9/15	9/22		
Ethan	9/17	9/23		
Ken	9/16	9/29	9/27	
La Toya	9/15	9/20		
Ireland	9/13	9/24		
Gabby	9/17	9/23		
James	9/15	9/22	9/27	
Davis	9/14	9/20		
Lilly	9/14	9/21		
Caleb	9/15	9/23		
Owen	9/14	9/21		
Ezekial	9/17	9/23		
Sarah	9/14	9/20		
Isaiah	9/17	9/21	9/27	

parts of the form, the conversations don't come to mind as clearly and I struggle to remember the work we did.

Teaching Point

A conference might take lots of directions, and no one way is the only right way. Because I have so many teaching options to choose from, I need to keep track of what I teach. These notes help me in later conferences when I contemplate my next teaching move. Many times I'll notice that a student has begun doing what I taught in our last conference, and I compliment her on following through. But if I notice that she is still struggling with this concept, I'll teach it in a different way.

Figure 3.12 Blank Anecdotal Record Sheet

STUDENT NAME:			
DATE/TITLE	**TEACHING POINT**	**OTHER POTENTIAL GOALS**	**MENTOR TEXT?**

Figure 3.12 Blank Anecdotal Record Sheet

Other Potential Goals

My goal in every conference is to teach the student the one most important thing that will help him not just in the current piece but in every piece he writes for rest of his life. I base this decision on all the things I value for learners and writers, everything I know about good writing, everything I know about student writers, and everything I know about this particular student. Although I teach only one thing in every conference, I notice other things the student needs help with. I jot down these other things I could have taught in this section. When I review the anecdotal record sheet before each conference, I consider whether now might be the right time to teach one of these other goals.

Mentor Text?

One way I ensure that every child's work is used in some way as a model for the group is by noting when I use the writing as a mentor text. I also keep track of the ways each child's work has been featured (lesson chart, strategy group, sharing session).

I'm usually able to identify student mentor texts easily, but teachers just beginning to confer with this kind of double lens might have trouble with it. If it is difficult for you to find student mentor texts, use your records to help you. Reread your anecdotal notes asking, "What did I teach in conferences today, or the last

Figure 3.13 A Completed Anecdotal Record Sheet for a Second Grader

Anecdotal Record Sheet

Student Name: Isaiah

Date/Title	Teaching Point	Goals	Mentor Text?
9/17 My Lost Tooth	★Great Lead! ✓Tie end to the beginning.	- More writing-volume! - Use ending punctuation.	Yes - Lead
9/21 Tag with James	✓Just starting piece, gave paper w/ more lines to increase volume.	- Plan before writing—touch, sketch, write	
9/27	✓Bring characters alive through talking (speech bubbles & words)	- Needs to add more details to pictures and words.	

May be photocopied for classroom use. © 2015 by Lisa Eickholdt from *Learning from Classmates: Using Students' Writing as Mentor Texts*. Portsmouth, NH: Heinemann.

few days, that I could bring to my lessons tomorrow?" Examine your records with this question in mind, and you will find many ways to use your students' writing in your teaching.

LET STUDENTS BE OUR GUIDE

Conferring with an eye toward identifying powerful elements in students' writing is really about taking advantage of the teachable moments that happen in our classrooms every day. Above all else, it is about letting our students guide our instructional decisions. It's about having plans but being flexible enough to adjust them to best meet our students' needs. Recently a teacher friend who uses her students' writing as mentor texts extensively in her teaching was discussing her lesson plans. "They're out on my desk as the administration requires, but I hope they don't look too closely at them! I make plans every week for what I'm teaching, but then I get in there and start teaching, and some kid does something so cool, so much better than what I had planned, I go with that instead!" This is really what it means to teach with our students' writing. When a kid does something really cool, we say, "That's great! Can you help me teach that in tomorrow's lesson?"

Things to keep in mind ----------------

Immersion

* Expose students to the genre: Immerse students before they write by reading lots of great mentor texts. This activity will give them a sense of the genre.

* Chart it: Work with students to highlight the key features of a genre. Post these on a class anchor chart.

* Choose wisely: Choose mentor texts that are filled with great craft so you can return to these same texts over and over again for different teaching points.

* Give a copy: Provide students with a copy of the mentor text to store in their writing folders. They can then return to the text over and over again as they are writing.

* Name it: Be sure to name the writing technique for students. Remember, naming something makes it repeatable.

* Don't assume compliance: Just because you tell students to do something, don't assume they will. Instead, help students understand why they should use a certain writing technique. Explain why it's effective. Show students how it will help them as writers or how it improves their writing.

Assessment

* Begin at the beginning: Assess your group of students before a unit of study so you can plan lessons that are responsive to their needs.

* Determine what you value: Decide what writing traits you value most. Then, search for these in your students' work.

* Choose a few teaching points: Decide what your students need to learn. Choose several goals for your group and plan lessons that support these goals.

* Search for student mentor texts: As you search for needs, search for possible mentor texts. Though many of your kids need help with a certain writing technique, there will be a few students who don't. Use these students' writing as mentor texts in your lessons.

* Repeat the process: Reassess your group midway through a unit to determine how best to meet students' current needs. Set new goals and create new lessons to support these needs.

* Reflect: Analyze your groups' writing after a study. Their writing is a mirror of your teaching. Reflect on how you can improve as a teacher.

Conferences

* Be optimistic: Examine your students' work with an eye toward the positive. Look beyond surface errors, and search for the good. Beautiful content often hides under tough-to-read handwriting.

* Confer with a double lens: As you work with individual students, keep your group in mind. Ask yourself, "What has this child done that he or she can teach the rest?"

* Record it: Write down anecdotal notes as you confer. Keep track of when you confer with each of your students, what you teach them, and how their writing was used as a mentor text.

* Honor all students: Be sure to use writing from each child in your class as a mentor text. Every child has something worthy to offer. Seek it out!

* Be flexible: Be ready to abandon your lesson plans when something better turns up. When a child does something amazing, be ready to shift gears and teach this wonderful new thing to everyone else.

Lessons

Power Teaching with Student Writing as a Mentor Text

With a room full of authors to help us, teaching writing doesn't have to be so lonely.

—*Katie Ray*

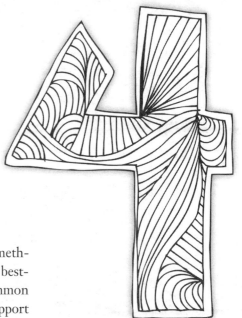

Many researchers have weighed in on what makes some instructional methods more effective than others, and several have recently emphasized best-practice instruction. Sampling the literature on best practice reveals some common themes. A key one is that instruction should begin with a high level of teacher support that is then gradually removed until students work independently (Anderson 2000; Calkins 2003; Harvey and Goudvis 2007). This is commonly known as the gradual release of responsibility (Pearson and Gallagher 1983). This model is sometimes explained in terms of the roles the teacher and students assume throughout instruction: I do (you watch); we do it (together); you do (I observe and assist); you do (I assess) (Pearson and Gallagher 1983).

My instruction is based on this model and adheres to the following progression: connect, teach, actively engage, and link (Anderson 2000; Calkins 2003). I begin every lesson by connecting the new writing work to students' ongoing work. I also explain why the strategy or writing concept is important for students to learn. I conclude the connection phase by stating the teaching point. In the teaching phase, I show students a piece of my writing and explain how I went about implementing this technique or use student mentor texts and, when possible, have the student writer describe his process. Seeing a developmentally appropriate model accompanied by step-by-step directions dramatically increases students' understanding. Next, I actively engage students, asking them to try out the new writing technique or strategy immediately within a supportive group environment. I end the lesson by reiterating the teaching point and providing another link to students' ongoing writing work. In addition to making my instruction meaningful and clear, following this model helps keep my instruction concise.

I try to keep a lesson to about ten minutes. The primary reason I keep it short is time management. I have between forty-five and sixty minutes a day for writing workshop. If the lesson takes longer than ten minutes, students get less time to write, and the only way students get better at writing is by writing—a lot! Knowing I have only a brief period to teach helps me keep my instruction focused. A short, focused lesson helps students maintain a high level of engagement.

Using a Lesson Planning Guide

Teaching using student mentor texts requires some additional decisions and considerations, and I use a lesson planning guide (see Figure 4.1) to help me.

Figure 4.1 Lesson Planning Guide for Using Student Writing

Month: Grade: Student Author/Mentor Text:

How will the mentor text be displayed?

Teaching point/goal:

Lesson explanation and introduction:
How?   *What?*   *Why?*

Type of demonstration:
Show and tell   *Before and after*   *Inquiry*   *Working backward*   *Peer editing*

Type of guided practice:
Student's writing   *Teacher's writing*   *Classmate's writing*   *Close study/discussion*

How Will the Mentor Text Be Displayed?

After I have identified a piece of student mentor text I want to use, I need to consider how to display it so that every student is able to see it clearly. Being able to both see and hear the mentor text increases students' understanding of and engagement with the text.

Enlarging mentor texts guarantees that they are readable. Ways to enlarge text include using a document camera, an LCD projector, or an overhead projector or rewriting the text on a chart. A document camera is easy to use and has the added benefit of allowing me to display the text in its original form. Another method is to project the mentor text onto a screen through my computer. Though this is more work—I have to scan the writing and save it in a file beforehand—the advantage is that I can share these files with other teachers (with the student author's permission) to use in their lessons as well. Since I began doing this a few years ago, my school's library of student mentor texts has grown substantially. Almost every week, I find a piece or two of student writing in my mailbox with a note from a teacher requesting I scan it for her.

Another way I ensure student mentor texts are easy to read is to make copies that students can keep in their writing folders. We can return to the same mentor text over and over as I point out various writing techniques the writer used in the piece. Students can write on these copies during the lesson, highlighting phrases, underlining sentences, starring words, or making notes in the margins.

Teaching Point/Goal

After deciding how to display the mentor text, I identify what I will be teaching my students—the goal of my instruction. Writing out my teaching point succinctly, in a sentence or two, is essential: Announcing it to my students focuses the lesson.

Lesson Explanation and Introduction

The explanation portion of the lesson is the beginning of group instruction. I tell how I discovered the student mentor text, giving the student author full credit for creating or deciding to use the writing technique. I also explain exactly what the students will be learning and why the strategy or technique will be useful to them.

Type of Demonstration

Because demonstrating is so critical to my instruction, I categorize my lessons based on the type of demonstration I will use. (The type I choose depends on my goals for instruction and the student mentor text I am using.)

- *Show and tell.* I use this method most often. I show the student text to the group and highlight the writing strategy or technique being used. After a short discussion, the students try out this method for themselves.

- *Before and after.* First I show a copy of the work before the writer tried the writing technique. Then I show the same piece after the technique has been applied. We then discuss the two pieces, noting exactly how the writing technique changed the writing for the better (made it more interesting, easier to envision, clearer, easier to read, and so on).

- *Inquiry.* An inquiry lesson is very different from the other types of lessons; the teaching is not explicit. Instead, I present a piece of student writing and lead students through the inquiry process (Ray 1999). There is a more guided practice but no demonstration as such. I begin by asking students what good things they notice about the text. They then discuss how what they noticed improved the writing and give the new technique a name (Ray 1999). Discovering a writing technique rather than being told about it makes the learning more meaningful.

- *Working backward.* Working backward is a unique way of teaching that is particularly effective when I want to teach students about planning. I display a completed piece of student text and ask the class to infer the plans the writer made before writing it. Students must read the text closely and understand the elements necessary to the genre. After the students have surmised what the plan was, the writer of the piece shares his or her actual plan.

- *Peer editing.* In a peer-editing lesson a member of the class presents her or his writing and requests help using a recently taught and demonstrated strategy; the other students then offer suggestions, practicing the strategy by assisting a peer.

Type of Guided Practice

Every lesson also includes a brief time in which my students practice what has just been demonstrated and explained. The four ways they can do this follow:

- *Try things out in their own writing.* I usually have students try out the technique in their own work. When they gather for the lesson, they bring their writing notebook, their writing folder, a pen or pencil, and a pack of sticky notes, so it's quick and easy for them to get out the piece they are currently working on and try out the new strategy.

- *Help me try things out in my writing.* Writing alongside my students provides an instant model. I pull out a piece I have been working on and ask students to help me try out the new technique. I say something like, "After I saw what Carlos did in his writing, I knew this was something I needed to do in mine. Take a look at my piece, and see if you can help me figure out how I might go about doing what Carlos did." This kind of practice is one of my kids' favorites, because they love helping their teacher. I use my writing as a model in each unit of study because I want the kids to see me write.

- *Help a classmate.* I assign students long-term writing partners throughout a unit of study (Calkins 2003). Having a consistent writing partner helps students get to know each other as writers. Writing partners sit together during lessons and share with each other at the end of workshop every day. In the lesson, one partner might try out the writing technique while the other assists, alternating the roles throughout the session.

- *Participate in a close study and discussion.* When a lesson doesn't lend itself to having students try out the new learning, I ask them to closely observe a writing technique and discuss what they noticed with their writing partner afterward. I make sure I tell them exactly what I expect: "As I read this section of the piece, I want you to notice how Josie put the reader in the character's shoes. Be ready to discuss exactly what she did, and why you think it was an effective writing technique." I often use this kind of guided practice during an inquiry lesson.

SCAFFOLDING STUDENT MENTORS

In a traditional classroom, the teacher usually does the demonstration (*I do, you watch*). However, in a classroom that uses student writing as mentor texts, the demonstration can also be conducted by "a more knowledgeable other" (Vygotsky 1978)—the student author. Though it's perfectly okay to use a student's writing with just an acknowledgment of the author—and students who are anxious about speaking in front of the class may prefer it and should be given this option—I usually ask the student to help me teach the lesson. My students see it as an honor and are thrilled their writing will be featured. But sometimes they need a little help. Ways I provide this scaffolding include the following:

- *Repeating back.* When students are explaining what they did, they sometimes lose track of their thoughts. Repeating what they just said usually helps them get back on course.

- *Questioning.* When students aren't providing enough information or direction in their explanation, I prompt them with questions: "What did you do first? What did you do next?"

- *Reminding*. When students forget exactly how they went about the writing task or overlook a step in the process, it helps to say something like, "I remember yesterday when we worked together you said or you did such-and-such."
- *Rephrasing*. After students explain what they did, I sometimes rephrase their "kid speak" in a more conventional way.
- *Reiterating*. If the other students cannot hear the mentor or aren't paying close attention, I reiterate what he or she has just said.
- *Listing*. As a student author is explaining his process, I often record the steps on a large piece of chart paper and then post it in the room as a visual reminder. (We may rehearse these steps during our conference to help the student author prepare.)

A Sample Show-and-Tell Lesson

Leslie and I sit at a table, a small stack of papers piled between us. We are assessing her fourth graders' initial on-demand narrative writing to create some early writing goals. The students understand focus, but they all struggle with elaboration, summarizing what happens instead of bringing moments alive. Portalupi and Fletcher (1998) suggest that a key way students can elaborate a narrative is by including scenes containing action, dialogue, and inner thoughts. We add creating scenes to our writing goals.

A couple of weeks later, during writing workshop, we have a conference with Jackson, who has just begun developing a notebook entry into a story about the big play he made in a baseball game. We read his first paragraph and discuss his intentions, which are to elaborate a succession of scenes. We teach him how to create a scene by weaving between action, thinking, and talking. After modeling how to do this, we leave him to work. At the end of workshop we check back with him. Impressed with the results, we ask Jackson to help us teach the other students this technique in the next day's lesson (see Figure 4.2).

Type of lesson: *Show and tell*

Month: *September*   Grade: *Fourth*   Student Author/Mentor Text: *Jackson/ "My Big Moment"*

How will the mentor text be displayed?
LCD and a photocopy for every student

Teaching point/goal:
Instead of summarizing every part of a story, writers build key sections into scenes containing action, thinking, and talking.

Lesson explanation and introduction:
Jackson was writing his second scene and wanted to bring that section alive by creating a scene that included three key elements: action, thinking, and talking.

Type of demonstration:
Show and tell

Type of guided practice:
Classmate's writing

Figure 4.2 Planning Guide for Show and Tell Lesson

Lesson Transcript

"Yesterday Leslie and I talked with Jackson. He is writing a story about the time he made a big play in a baseball game. As we were talking, he realized something important—he was summarizing the scenes in his story instead of elaborating them. Writers do summarize some parts of their story. However, they bring the important parts alive. One way to do this is to present these parts as scenes, like a movie, and then bring these scenes to life through action, thinking, and talking. Writers, one goal we have for our stories is to make readers feel they are right there with us, reliving our experience. In order to do that, we need to build scenes. Today Jackson is going to teach us how to do this. Let's look at the chart I made about building scenes. [*I display the following chart.*]

Writers build key parts of their stories into scenes by including:

- Action
  - Describing what the character is doing (outside story)

- Thinking
  - Describing what the character is thinking or feeling (inside story)

- Talking
  - Making the character talk (dialogue)

"On the whiteboard you see Jackson's piece; I also gave you a photocopy. He is going to read the first two paragraphs to you. Afterward, we'll look at how he built the second paragraph into scenes. [*Jackson reads the first part of his story—Figure 4.3— to the class, and the students applaud.*]

"Okay, writers, I want you to watch as I reread the second paragraph in Jackson's story. After each sentence I read, I am going to pause, and Jackson is going to label the technique he used to build this part into a scene. You follow along as we do this. Let's start. [*I read aloud, pausing after each sentence. Jackson labels each sentence as action, thinking, or talking, as appropriate.*]

"Did you notice how he used all three elements to build this scene? And didn't you feel you were right there with him on base with two strikes against you? This is why we do this, so readers feel they're right there with us—like they're walking in the character's shoes, as we say in reading workshop. Now it's your turn. I want you to work on the next paragraph in his piece. Read that paragraph, and do exactly what we just did here together. I want you and your partner to read it over and label each sentence by putting letters off to the side—*a* for action, *th* for thinking or feelings, and a *t* for talking. [*Student pairs discuss and label each sentence. Jackson and I listen*

My big moment

One cold night, I was going up to Bogan Park to play baseball. I was so ready to get my hands dirty on the ball field. There was just one problem. My good friend, Davis, was playing me that night. He was on the Cubs, one of the hardest teams to face. But that night, I had a feeling, a feeling different than any other. I felt very determined, and competitive that night. I felt that something good was going to come up.

Finally, it was game time. I still had all that confidence in me. My team was up to bat, and guess who had to start off? I was ready to bust the guts off of that ball. The pitcher threw the first pitch. "STRIKE ONE!!" the umpire yelled. "OK, shake it off," I said. The pitcher threw one right down the middle, and I swung. "STRIKE TWO!!" the umpire yelled. I started to whisper to myself, "Oh man, I might strikeout! Well, I will do my best, this is my time, I need to go big or go home.

The pitcher threw the ball right down the middle. Right speed, right place. WHACK!!! It went so far, it touched the fence in the air. I quickly ran to first base, and looked at the first base coach to get my sign as I rounded second base. I rushed to third base. My dad was waiting for me at third. "Go home, you can make it!!"

my dad said. Those words ran through my head over and over again. I started thinking, "What if I don't make it? What if I let down my team and loose the game?"

I ran with all my might. I felt like I was an out of control train. There was no turning back now. I feel proud that I've gone this far... but can I make an inside the park homerun? My heart was beating as fast as it could. Then, I was thinking I could run the catcher over so he would miss the catch. That was the only thing I could do, so I gave it a shot.

I jumped hard with my foot in front of me, and I slid. I did not know what happened. I opened my eyes. My plan worked! The catcher got knocked down and let go of the ball. "Jackson, touch home!" my dad said. He was right. I didn't touch home. I dove for home plate. My palm covered home plate like a blanket. "SAFE!" the umpire called out. Everyone started to go nuts. I hugged my dad, and high fived my teamates. I was right! I just knew something good was going to happen!

in, guiding and helping as needed. *After a few minutes, we come back together and reach consensus as a group.*]

"Remember, when you want to bring a scene alive in a story, one way writers do that is by including action, thinking, and talking. If you do that today, let me know. I'd like to see it. Now, off you go!"

Later that day I work with Trinity, who tells me she is drafting her story into scenes like Jackson had. Reading her draft (Figure 4.4), I see immediately that he has indeed influenced her writing. However, her story focuses on an internal struggle (her nervousness to run a long race for the first time), and she emphasizes the "inside story." Students need to know that they can focus on one of the scene-building elements more than the others, depending on what they want to emphasize.

Figure 4.4 Trinity, Fourth Grade, "My First 1500"

My First 1500

One lovely, early morning, my dad, my two brothers, and I all flew to Tennesee to compete in a track meet. My brothers and I were all planning to run. The sun was just waking up and everyone was excited about running their race. I was biting my nails and lots of what ifs were racing through my mind.

What if I don't finish the race? I thought. What if I trip and fall? What if I come in last place? I usually ran short sprints, but I was scheduled to run a 1500! That is about 1 mile. Everytime I thought about my race (which happened a lot) my stomach seemed to tighten. And two short sentences kept running through my mind—Why today? Why now?

We landed and thoughts were still racing around in my mind.

My dad said, "Just focus on your race."

I could easily focus on my race, just in a...

not so good way. I really tried to imagine myself winning the race, but it was not easy. By the time I run my race, I thought, I won't have any more nails to chew on!

As soon as I got on the starting line, my stomach was in knots like crazy! I wished I could just dissapear. On the bright side, my nails survived my teeth for a few hours. I knew I was scared, but I had to concentrate.

I kept my eyes locked to the track not daring to look into the eyes of the people I was racing.

"Runners, take your marks," said the starter. I took a deep breath. POW! The race was off!

I was trying so hard to stay with the pack, but my "what ifs" were holding me back. Suddenly, I had remembered what my dad had said.

"Just focus on your race."

I kept repeating those words in my head. I was starting to slowly calm down. Finally, I was

completly focused. Infact, I was so focused, it didn't occur to me what place I was in. I looked up and no one was infront of me. I knew this could only mean one thing. I was in first place!

I was so happy that I got an extra boost of courage to keep going. I was exhausted, but I kept going. I was almost there. Then, I saw it. The finish line.

I started sprinting to the finish line. My dad was cheering me on. Stubby nails and all, I had done it! I had won my first 1500!

As soon as I passed that finish line, it was almost like the world stopped. Then 1 person started clapping. Then 2, 4, and soon, the whole stadium was cheering!

I learned that very moment that you may suprise yourself on what you can accomplish, and if you work up to something, nothing is impossible.

A Sample Before-and-After Lesson

I'm working as a writing consultant in a very small rural school district in Colorado; fewer than two hundred kids are in the whole district. The third-grade class I'm visiting has recently begun a study on opinion writing. The students began this unit by writing, with their teacher, a letter to the school board requesting new playground equipment. Now they are drafting pieces of their own.

Writers support their opinions by including facts, quotes, numbers, and anecdotes (Calkins and Gillette 2006). Calling anecdotes *ministories* makes it easier for kids to remember. In this lesson, I'm teaching students to create better introductions to their letters by using a ministory to explain why they chose their topic. I use the before-and-after structure because I hope seeing a dry lead become more interesting will prompt them to try this technique (see Figure 4.5).

Type of lesson: *Before and after*

Month: *March*   Grade: *Third*   Student Author/Mentor Text: *Natalia/"Pocket Squirrel" Lead*

How will the mentor text be displayed?
Chart paper

Teaching point/goal:
One way to introduce an opinion piece is to tell the story of how you got your idea.

Lesson explanation and introduction:
Argument/opinion writers introduce their topic to their reader and state their opinion. Telling a ministory is a great way to do this.

Type of demonstration:
Before and after

Type of guided practice:
Student's own writing

Figure 4.5 Planning Guide for Before and After Lesson

Lesson Transcript

"Good morning, writers! I'm so happy to be here working with you today. I can't believe I saw deer walking in town! I understand that's pretty normal around here. You guys see deer all the time, don't you? [*The kids smile and nod.*] I am also so excited because I heard we're going to get a lot of snow tonight—like fifteen inches! I can't wait! I live in Georgia, and we don't get snow very much at all. And we've never gotten fifteen inches of snow at one time. [*Starting to relax, the kids tell me stories about playing in the snow.*]

"Let's get started. I understand that you all have just started writing opinion pieces. And your teacher showed me the letter you wrote to the school board about getting some new playground equipment. You did such a great job! I think that when you send this to the board they're going to be very impressed with your writing, and they just may buy you some new equipment because of it. Good work!

As I read through your letter, I noticed you started by listing all the reasons you need new equipment. You said things like it's old, and because it's old some parts are broken or rusty. Then, later in the letter you told more about each of these reasons. That's one way to start an opinion or argument piece. You can begin by listing all the reasons you believe you need something. But today I want to teach you another way to start an opinion piece that I think is a little more interesting. I call it using a ministory. Let me show you what I mean.

"Here is a piece of writing from one of my third-grade students. We were writing opinion pieces a couple of months ago, and Natalia decided she wanted to write a letter to her parents to convince them to get her a pet—a pocket squirrel. I had never heard of such an animal. Sometimes they're called sugar gliders. Have any of you ever heard of them? Turn and talk to your elbow partner for a minute. [*Kids turn and talk, and we share a few things as a group.*] Okay, a lot of you have heard of these pets. Interesting. Now I want to show you Natalia's first lead to her letter [*Figure 4.6*]. I wrote it on a chart so we can all see it. I'll read it aloud, and you follow along.

"Do you see how Natalia just listed all the reasons she wants a pocket squirrel? That's okay, but I think she could make her introduction a lot more interesting if she told the story of how she decided she wanted this little guy for a pet. So that's

Figure 4.6 Natalia's First Lead, Third Grade

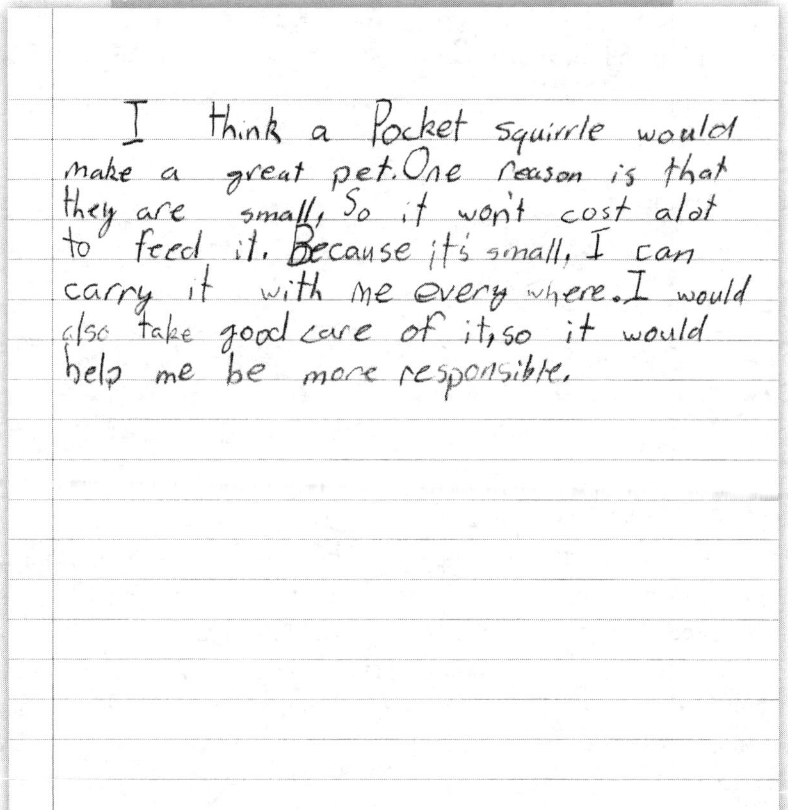

I think a Pocket squirrle would make a great pet. One reason is that they are small, So it won't cost alot to feed it. Because it's small, I can carry it with me every where. I would also take good care of it, so it would help me be more responsible.

what Natalia did. She rewrote her introduction and told the story about how she came up with this idea. Let's look at her second version [*Figure 4.7*] and compare her two leads. After we read her new lead, turn and talk to your partner about the two introductions. What do you think about them? Which one is more interesting?

[*After we read both leads, the kids turn and talk, and I listen in.*] "I heard a lot of you say that the second lead is a lot more interesting. I heard you say that it was also more convincing. I agree. Telling the story about how and when you came up with your idea is very powerful. I call this using a ministory, and it's something writers do all the time when they write opinion or argument pieces. You can use it in your lead, like we saw here, or you can use it to support one of your reasons.

"Now it's your turn. I want you to think about your topic and how you could start by telling the story of when you got the idea, like Natalia did. How might that go? Think for a minute. [*I allow some wait time.*] Turn and tell your partner how that might go. [*The kids turn and talk, and I listen in.*] I heard Shawn talking about how this might work for him. Shawn, would you share with the rest of the group what you told your partner, please?"

Shawn says, "Yes. I said that I am writing about how we need to help the homeless more. I got the idea because one day we were driving in town, and I looked

Figure 4.7 Natalia's Lead Using a Ministory

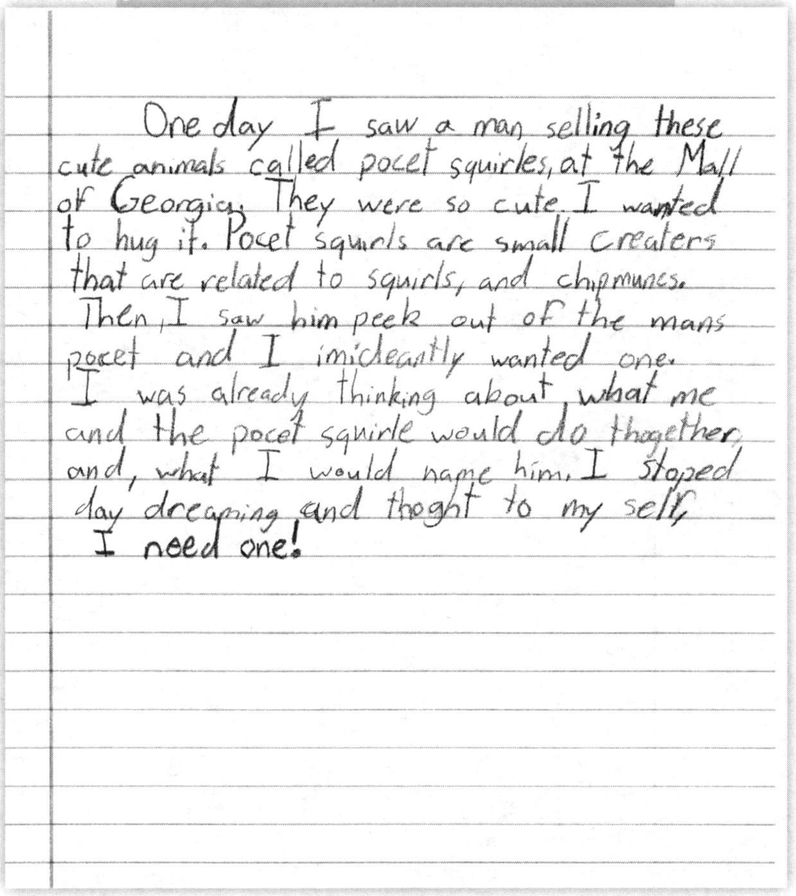

One day I saw a man selling these cute animals called pocet squirles, at the Mall of Georgia. They were so cute. I wanted to hug it. Pocet squirls are small creaters that are related to squirls, and chipmunes. Then, I saw him peek out of the mans pocet and I imideantly wanted one. I was already thinking about what me and the pocet squirle would do thogether, and, what I would name him. I stoped day dreaming and thoght to my self, I need one!

May be photocopied for classroom use. © 2015 by Lisa Eickholdt from *Learning from Classmates: Using Students' Writing as Mentor Texts*. Portsmouth, NH: Heinemann.

up and saw someone dump a drink out of his window onto something in the ditch. When we drove by I looked closer and saw it was a person. Those people dumped soda all over a homeless guy who was sitting in the ditch! And I thought that was really wrong—we need to help the homeless, not hurt them!" [*The room grows silent for a minute as we all think about Shawn's story.*]

"Wow. What a sad story. Hearing that story is so heartrending. I think everyone in here was moved by your words, Shawn. Thanks for sharing. [*I let the silence hang in the room for a moment.*] So, writers, one way to start your opinion pieces is by simply and honestly telling the story of how you got the idea—exactly like we saw Natalia do in her piece, and exactly like we heard Shawn do. A ministory is also a good thing to use any time you want to tell more about one of your reasons. Today as you go off to write, think about whether using a ministory in your lead is something you want to try. I'll be coming around and can't wait to see what you're all working on! Now, off you go!"

The kids respond well to this lesson. They write about issues like horsewhipping, the homeless, and poaching (topics very different from the ones I'm used to, living in the suburbs). Jenna's lead about poaching, which I think is poignant, is shown in Figure 4.8.

Figure 4.8 Jenna's Ministory Lead to Her Piece on Poaching, Third Grade

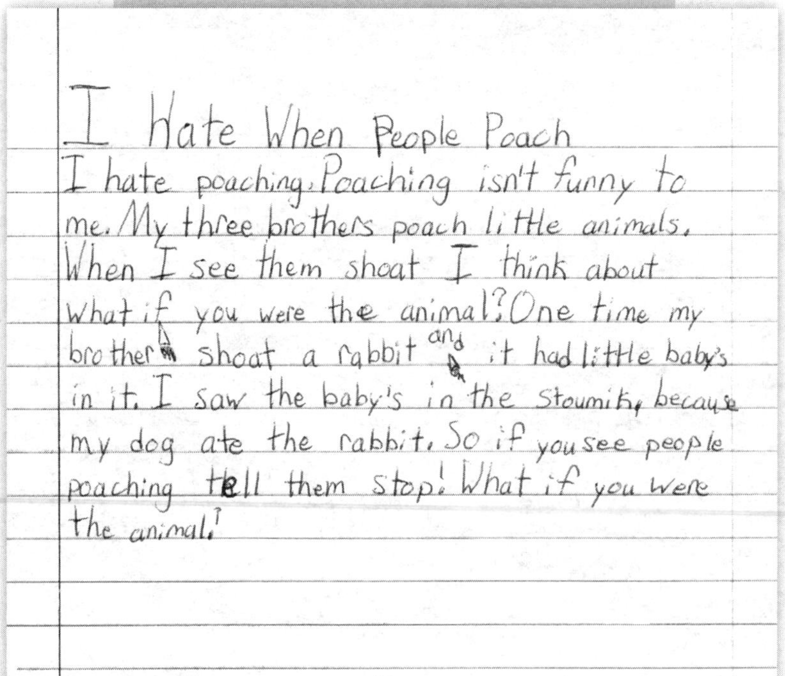

> I Hate When People Poach
> I hate poaching. Poaching isn't funny to me. My three brothers poach little animals. When I see them shoat I think about what if you were the animal? One time my brother shoat a rabbit and it had little baby's in it. I saw the baby's in the stoumik, because my dog ate the rabbit. So if you see people poaching tell them stop! What if you were the animal?

A Sample Inquiry Lesson

I'm working in a third-grade classroom in which the students are nearing the end of a unit on informational writing. The students are writing books about things they already know a lot about. I've noticed in my assessments that most of them jump right into their topic with little thought of capturing the readers' interest. I use a couple of second graders' pieces with more interesting beginnings as mentor texts in an inquiry lesson (see Figure 4.9).

Type of lesson: *Inquiry*

Month: *November*   Grade: *Third*   Student Author/Mentor Text: *Gianna/"Meet Tornado";*
Jack/"Meet the Sharks";
Ashley/Introduction to
"Snakes Fantastic"

Figure 4.9 Planning Guide for Inquiry Lesson

How will the mentor text be displayed?
Photocopies for each child

Teaching point/goals:
Informational writers include an introduction before jumping into their topic.

Lesson explanation and introduction:
I've been reading over your informational books and noticed that you all need to include an introduction to your topic.

Type of demonstration:
Inquiry lesson: no demonstration, extended guided practice

Type of guided practice:
Classmate's writing/student's own writing

Lesson Transcript

"Writers, I have been reading your informational books over the last few days and am so impressed! You all have done a wonderful job of teaching your readers all about your topic. I now know so much more about baseball, soccer, and dogs than I ever knew before I read your writing! Great job! But I've also noticed something else about your books. Most of you just jump into your topics without any kind of introduction. In our last unit on narrative writing, we learned that it's important to begin your writing in a way that captures your readers' attention. In an informational book you will want to do the same thing. You'll want to write an interesting beginning that introduces the reader to your topic. This will help grab their attention. Today you're going to learn how to revise your writing by adding an introduction.

"We're going to do something different, though. We're going to be researchers. We've done this before, so I know you all can do this. I've given you each a copy of three book introductions written by some kids at our school. [*I leave out the fact that they are second graders.*] We're going to read these beginnings closely and research exactly what the writers did to introduce their topics to their readers. Let's start by looking at the one called "Meet the Tornado," by Gianna [*Figure 4.10*] and the one called "Meet the Shark," by Jack [*Figure 4.11*]. Both writers use the same writing technique in their introduction. Let's read these like researchers and see if we can notice and name what these writers did. Read along in your head as I read them aloud.

"Okay, turn and talk to your partner. What did you notice about both of these introductions? What did the writers do? [*The kids turn and talk for a few minutes, and I listen in.*] "I heard you all say that both of these introductions start with the word *meet*. One begins, "Meet the Tornado," and the other, "Meet the Shark." That's one obvious way they're alike, but I want you to look at the writing under the heading. What did the writers do that's the same there? Turn and talk. [*The students turn and talk for a few minutes, and I listen in.*]

"I listened to Alicia and her partner. Alicia, tell the group what you noticed about the writing?"

"We noticed that both of them told a little story," Alicia says.

"Thumbs up if you and your partner noticed that both of these pieces told a little story. [*Lots of thumbs go up.*] Interesting. Alicia, what else did you notice about the stories?"

"Well, it's not a big story," Alicia says, "but just a little exciting part of a story."

"Wow! Anyone else notice that? [*Heads nod all over the room.*] Let's think about what we might call this way of introducing a topic. Opening with action? Opening with a scene? Turn and talk to your partner. [*I listen in.*]

"I heard most of you say you want to call this technique opening with a scene. [*I add this to our chart.*] We talked about scenes in our last narrative unit, didn't we? Writers, I want you to think about the informational book you're writing. How could you try beginning with a scene like Gianna and Jack did? [*I wait while the kids*

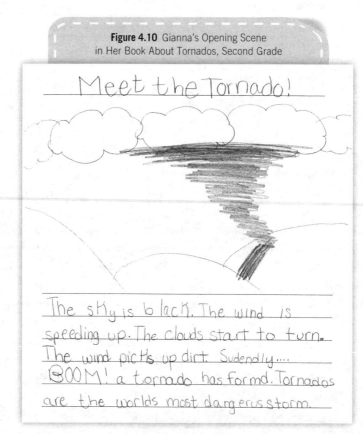

Figure 4.10 Gianna's Opening Scene in Her Book About Tornados, Second Grade

Meet the Tornado!

The sky is black. The wind is speeding up. The clouds start to turn. The wind pickts up dirt. Sudendly.... BOOM! a tornado has formd. Tornados are the worlds most dangerous storm.

Figure 4.11 Jack's Opening Scene
in His Book About Sharks, Second Grade

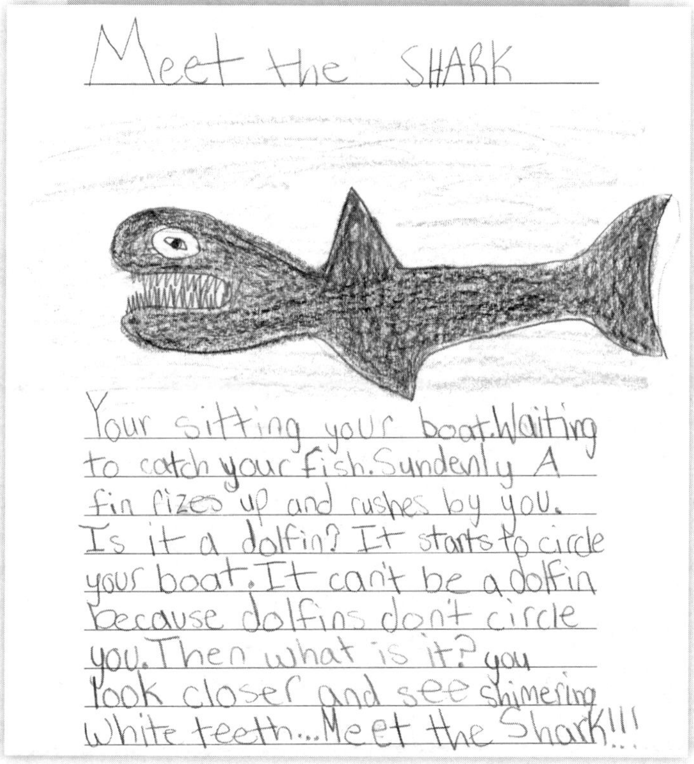

Meet the SHARK

Your sitting your boat.Waiting to catch your fish. Sundenly A fin rizes up and rushes by you. Is it a dolfin? It starts to circle your boat. It can't be a dolfin because dolfins don't circle you. Then what is it? you look closer and see shimering white teeth...Meet the Shark!!!

think.] Now turn and tell your partner how that might go. Partner one, you go first. [*The kids turn and talk.*]

"Writers, I heard a lot of great opening scenes. Today when you go off to write, you might want to try adding an introduction in which you create a scene like Gianna and Jack did. But before you leave, I want to show you one other way you might want to introduce your topic to your reader. Take out the other mentor text I gave you that has the heading "Introduction" [*Figure 4.12*]. You probably remember this book. We read it when we were first learning about informational texts. This time we'll read it like researchers and see what Ashley did to introduce you to her topic. Follow along as I read it aloud."

The students repeat the process of inquiry. They notice and name what Ashley did in her piece: wrote a letter that told the story of why she chose her topic. Then they envision how this technique might work in their own writing and share it with their partner.

"So now you know two different ways you could introduce your topic to your reader. You could open with a scene, or you could write a letter to the reader that tells the story of why you decided to write about your topic. Or you might come up with a whole new kind of introduction, maybe one you've seen in other mentor texts or learned about in other classes. But here's the thing: Most informational writers introduce their topics to the reader in some way to catch their interest. So if you try one of these techniques today, let me know. I want to see it. Or if you come up with a whole new kind of introduction, I want to see that too. Off you go!"

The kids respond beautifully to this lesson. They use ideas from all the mentor texts, sometimes combining methods, to create their own unique beginnings. See the examples in Figures 4.13, 4.14, 4.15, and 4.16.

Figure 4.12 Ashley's Introductory Letter, Second Grade

Introduction

Dear reader, The reason I chosed these topic is becase, When I was about 7 years old I went to a zoo and found a sign that said (baby snakes loose in the zoo! Be carful!) And when we come in I come face to face with one. And I picked it up and it did not bit me! It was werid becase snakes usalcy bite. I asked my mom and dad if I could keep it and they said if you spend all the money for it so I did and I named him scales. Thats why I picked this topic.

Love, Ashley. I

Figure 4.13 Connor's Lead to His Book About Baseball, Third Grade

Introduction

Dear Reader,

The reason I picked this topic is because when I was 6, I started playing baseball. It was the second game of the season. I was the catcher. The pitcher jetted the ball towards my glove. the batter hit it, he went to first, then to second, and then third, then he came home to me. and The third base men threw the ball to me. I tagged the runner out for the win. Everey body on my team came at me and gave me hi fives. I was very exided. That is why I wrote this book.

From,
Connor

①

Figure 4.14 Alexia's Lead to Her Book About Soccer, Third Grade

Introduction

Dear Reader,

The reason I chose the topic soccer is because once my mom told me about her soccer life. She told me about how she played in highschool and college. She told me about winning games and how she loved it. I decided to follow my mom's footsteps so I went to soccer camp.

At soccer camp I learned how to jugle the ball, pass the ball and shoot the ball. My mom was right it was so fun at soccer camp.

-1-

Figure 4.15 Alicia's Lead to
Her Book About Softball, Third Grade

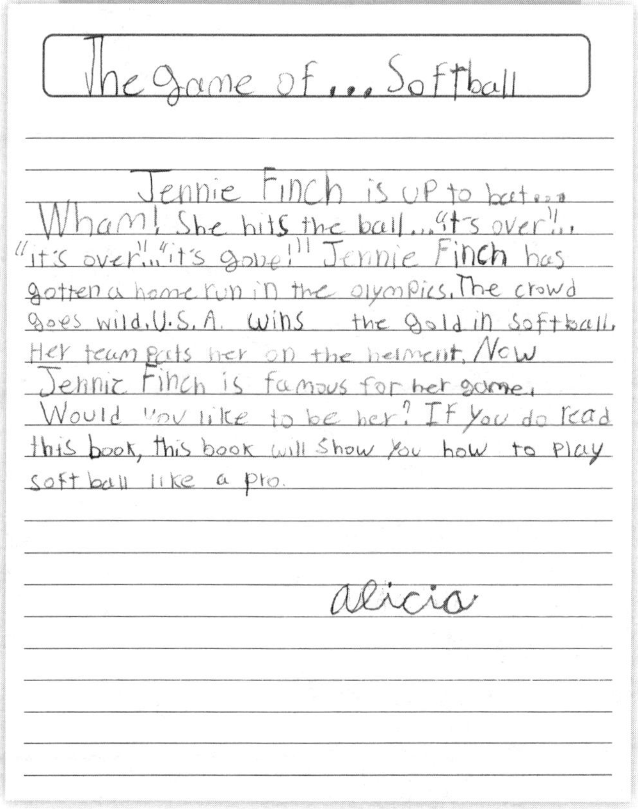

The game of ... Softball

Jennie Finch is up to bat... Wham! She hits the ball..."It's over"... "It's over"..."it's gone!" Jennie Finch has gotten a home run in the olympics. The crowd goes wild. U.S.A. wins the gold in softball. Her team puts her on the helmcnt. Now Jennie Finch is famous for her game. Would you like to be her? If you do read this book, this book will show you how to play softball like a pro.

alicia

Figure 4.16 Parker's Lead to
His Book About Football, Third Grade

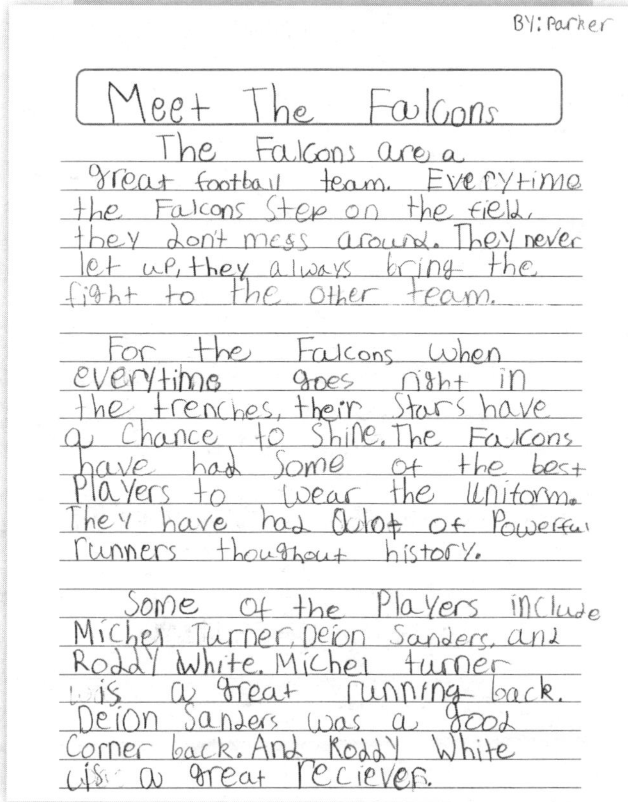

BY: Parker

Meet The Falcons

The Falcons are a great footbal team. Everytime the Falcons step on the field, they dont mess around. They never let up, they always bring the fight to the other team.

For the Falcons when everytime goes right in the trenches, their stars have a chance to shine. The Falcons have had some of the best players to wear the uniform. They have had alot of powerful runners thoughout history.

Some of the players include Michel Turner, Deion Sanders, and Roddy White. Michel turner is a great running back. Deion Sanders was a good corner back. And Roddy White is a great reciever.

A SAMPLE WORKING-BACKWARD LESSON

It's important to teach students to make a plan before they write. At our school, we teach older students (grades 3 through 5) to use graphic organizers for this step. Our favorite graphic organizer for informational and opinion writing is one we call boxes and bullets (adapted from Calkins and Gillette 2006). It is easy to draw and simple to use. Laura has assessed her fifth graders' writing and noticed a lot of unorganized and underdeveloped paragraphs. She has taught them how to use a boxes-and-bullets graphic organizer to plan and feels they need more instruction. Hoping to shed a new light on this writing strategy, she conducts a working-backward lesson (see Figure 4.17).

Lesson Transcript

"Lately we've been talking about the upcoming writing test. For one thing, we want to make sure we have a plan before we draft, so we've been reviewing some of the graphic organizers we can use. However, I've noticed that a lot of you aren't making any kind of plan before you write. Because you're not planning, your paragraphs aren't organized and developed. Today we're going to learn more about planning and elaborating our paragraphs using boxes and bullets. We're also going to see how we can use the plan to develop our writing. Here's a paragraph from Madeline's informational essay about how to use an educational web site [*Figure 4.18*]. Let's see what we can learn from her. [*She distributes the copies, then reads the paragraph aloud.*]

"I just love this piece! Great job, Madeline. Today, we're going to think about how Madeline planned this part of her essay. We're going to work backward from

Figure 4.17 Planning Guide for Working Backward

Type of lesson: *Working backward*

Month: *February*　　Grade: *Fifth*　　Student Author/Mentor Text: *Madeline/Essay Paragraph*

How will the mentor text be displayed?

Photocopies

Teaching point/goal:

Writers make plans before they write and elaborate their writing based on these plans.

Lesson explanation and introduction:

Planning helps writers organize and elaborate their writing into well-developed paragraphs.

Type of demonstration:

Working backward

Type of guided practice:

Classmate's writing

Figure 4.18 Madeline's Informational Paragraph, Fifth Grade

Teacher: Theftford

Name: Madeline

What things you need to do to sign in and create an account and password. You might want to do something easy to remember like your name or maybe something funny. Here is an example, you might chose the word pumpkin. If you do not like that method, you can use the most common method: write it down and hide it. Be sure you hide it where you can remember, and where nobody can find it. If you don't hide it, they can go on your account and hack it or change it. Next, you create an ID. First you chose a character. Second, you type in your first name or a name you want your charachter to have. Third you have to put in your grade and age. That way the computer can get the right information. Last, you click on on the bar that says what I am learning. Now type in the part you are leaning. Say you are leaning about the Blue Ridge Mountains. A bunch of facts should have popped up. From there, you would see a box that says play game. Click that to start playing the game. To recap it all, that is how you would sign in.

her completed paragraph and consider how her plan probably looked before she wrote it. This will help us understand how to use boxes and bullets in our own work. Right now I want you to open your notebooks to a clean page and draw a boxes-and-bullets organizer. Just draw one pair of boxes, since we're only focusing on her first paragraph. I'm going to do the same thing. [*She draws the following organizer on a large piece of chart paper.*]

THESIS STATEMENT: How to use an educational web site.	
Main Idea	*Supporting Details*

"We can fill in her thesis statement, because we know what it is. Our focus is on how she planned this paragraph. We're going to try to determine her main idea and supporting details. I'm going to reread her paragraph again and think about her main idea. It should be obvious, because every sentence should support her main idea in some way. [*She rereads the piece.*] Everything is about how to set up an account. I also noticed she announces her main idea in the first sentence of the piece as writers often do. Turn and talk to your partner. Do you agree? [*Students turn and talk as Laura listens in.*] Okay, it seems like you all agree with me. Madeline, am I right? Was this your main idea for this part? [*Madeline says yes.*] Great! Can you fill in the first box on our chart for us, please? Everyone else go ahead and jot the main idea down on your paper too.

THESIS STATEMENT: How to use an educational web site.	
Main Idea • How to set up an account.	*Supporting Details*

"Now it's your turn. I want you to work with your partner and see if you can figure out the first two supporting details, or bullets, that Madeline used in this paragraph. When you do, write them down on your graphic organizer. I want you to notice when Madeline begins a new detail. See if you can do this. You'll need to reread the paragraph again and talk about it with your partner. [*Laura listens in and guides the students as they work.*] I see that most of you have written down the same thing that I have on my graphic organizer. Madeline, are we right? Were these your first two supporting details? [*Madeline says yes.*]

THESIS STATEMENT: How to use an educational web site.	
Main Idea • How to set up an account.	*Supporting Details* • Sign in and create a password. • Create an ID.

"I want you to notice something. Look at how she elaborated each supporting detail. This whole first part is all about thinking of a password and tips on how to do that. And this whole next part is all about creating an ID. Remember, you jot down your bullets, and then you blow them up, just as we see Madeline doing here. That's how you elaborate. Now I want you to figure out her final supporting detail. Try this on your own, and when you think you have it figured out, write it down. [*She supports the kids as they work.*]

"Writers, can I have your attention? Here is what I noticed most of you have written down. Maybe you haven't used the same words I did, but you all thought the last supporting detail was something similar to what I jotted down. Right? Okay, turn and talk to your partner, and tell them what you're thinking about this piece.

THESIS STATEMENT: How to use an educational web site.	
Main Idea • How to set up an account.	*Supporting Details* • Sign in and create a password. • Create an ID. • Choose what you want to learn about.

"I heard a lot of you say you couldn't believe how long this one box-and-bullet section was when it was written out. I agree, it is long, and that's one thing I really love about this paragraph! I love how Madeline told us a lot about each supporting detail! She didn't tell us just one or two sentences about each one; she elaborated. When you go off today, think about Madeline's piece, and make your plan using boxes and bullets before you write. You will want to keep this mentor text next to you while you work."

After this lesson, Jonathan plans and writes a paragraph for his argumentative essay on why having a water park closer to his neighborhood would be good for kids. See Figure 4.19.

Figure 4.19 Jonathan's Box-and-Bullets Plan and Paragraph, Fifth Grade

> kids will get healthier | • swimming around
> • all the kids walking to different areas
> • kids would go to the water park instead of whatching tv
>
> If you buld a water park near us, kids will get healthier.
> Kids will finally get of their couch and go to the water park! Instead of the alternitive choice, eating chips and watching tv. They, us kids, will go to that park and swim, when you swim you burn fat and gain muscle in your arm and legs. Plus all the kids walking around will burn fat. Did you know that on average kids walk 5 miles at the water park? That is kinda long if you ask me. This would help stop childhood obesity in Gwinnett.

A SAMPLE PEER-EDITING LESSON

I'm working with kindergartners on a poetry unit. I have recently taught the children how to make comparisons (use similes and metaphors) in their poems, and many students have begun to do this. I've also taught a lesson on keeping a comparison going within a poem (see Figure 4.20).

Lesson Transcript

"Recently we've been talking about making comparisons in our poems. We learned comparisons can really help us show our readers what we mean. For example, when our classroom gets really cold, we said we could compare the coldness of the room to feeling like winter. Then we learned that if we make a comparison, it's a good idea to continue to use it throughout the poem. If the classroom feels as cold as winter, we could keep that comparison going by saying, 'We huddle together reading, the books keeping us warm.' At the end of workshop yesterday I was talking to Graham about his poem. As we read it together, he realized that he had made a lot of different comparisons in his poem instead of making one and continuing it. Then he did something really smart: He asked me for help. Graham wants to revise his poem and make it better, but he's not sure how to do that. So today we're all going to help Graham make his poem better. Let me read you what he has so far. [*I read Graham's poem, Figure 4.21.*]

"Do you see how he starts by comparing the clouds to soft pillows in the sky, but then he changes and compares them to ice cream and finally to marshmallows? He made a lot of different comparisons, instead of choosing one and sticking with it. Writers, Graham has asked for our help. So today we're all going to be his writing partners. We're going to give him some suggestions on how he might continue a comparison in his poem. Remember how we did this work yesterday? First, we thought of winter and all the things we do like huddling around a fire to keep warm.

Type of lesson: *Peer editing*

Month: *April*   Grade: *Kindergarten*   Student Author/Mentor Text: *Graham/"Clouds"*

How will the mentor text be displayed?
Chart paper

Teaching point/goal:
Poets make a comparison and keep the comparison going throughout a poem (Heard 1999).

Lesson explanation and introduction:
Graham requested help with his poem yesterday, and all of us are going to help him revise his poem so he can keep his comparison going.

Type of demonstration:
None; extended guided practice

Type of guided practice:
Classmate's writing

Figure 4.20 Planning Guide for Peer Editing Lesson

Figure 4.21 Graham's Poem "Clouds" Before Peer Editing

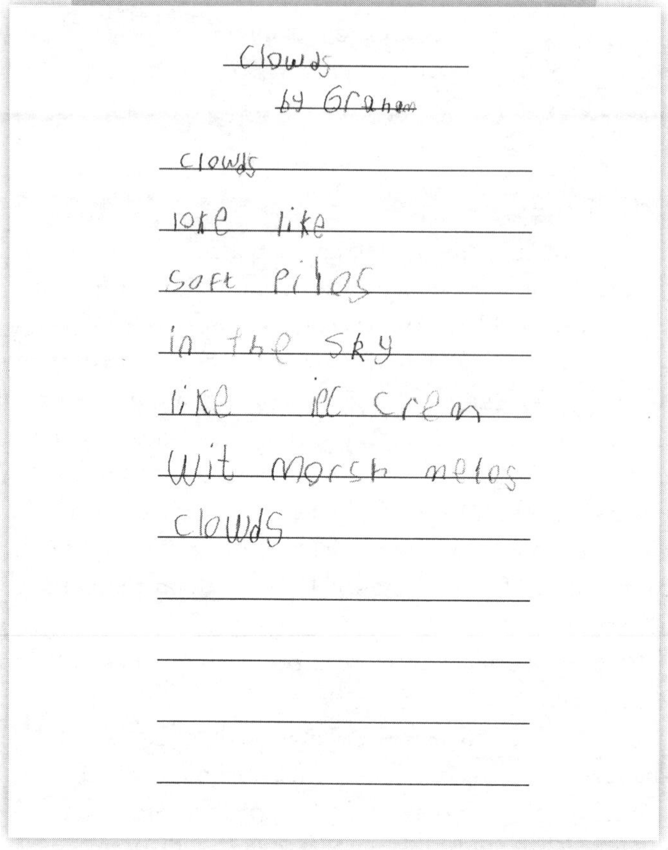

Clouds
by Graham

clouds

look like

soft piles

in the sky

like ic crem

wit marsh melos

clouds

Then, we thought about how we might do something similar in our classroom. You will want to do that same work right now.

"Graham has made several comparisons, and he likes them all, but today we're going to see if we can help him compare clouds to ice cream. You'll want to think about how clouds and ice cream might be the same. Then think about other lines he might add to keep up this idea. Let's all just think for a minute about how clouds might be like ice cream. Let's think about the things we know about ice cream and the things we do with ice cream. How are clouds like ice cream? [*I pause and let the students think.*] Turn and talk to your partner. [*Graham and I listen in as the students discuss various possibilities.*]

"As Graham and I were listening in we heard some great suggestions. Graham, what was one of the suggestions you heard?"

Graham replies, "Parker said I could say, 'The white clouds are like vanilla ice cream and the dark clouds are like chocolate.'"

"Oh, clever! I like it! Parker, did you mean the chocolate clouds are like storm clouds? You know how the clouds get dark when it rains?"

"Yeah! Like thunder clouds!" Parker says.

"If we were to keep up with that idea, what else could we say about the chocolate and vanilla clouds? Turn and talk to your partner. [*Students suggest things like the rain could be chocolate sauce making puddles on the ground and the thunder could be sprinkles.*] Graham, what were some suggestions you heard about this idea?"

"Sarah said the chocolate thunder cloud sounds like an ice cream cone getting crunched," Graham replies.

"So you might say that the clouds look like ice cream and then talk about something in the sky crunching the cone? Maybe a bird is up there eating the cone and making it sound like thunder? Then you might add on to that idea? [*Graham nods.*] Do you feel ready to try this poem again on your own then? [*Graham nods.*] Okay, let us know when you've rewritten your poem. We can't wait to see how it turns out! Thanks, Graham!

"Poets, one of the jobs of a poet is to help the reader see things in a new way, and making comparisons is one way to do that. Remember that if you're going to make a comparison in your poem, you'll want to think about keeping the same comparison going from the beginning of the poem all the way to the end. If you are going to do that kind of work today, please call me over. I'd love to see it. Off you go!"

Graham revises his poem (see Figure 4.22) but decides not to use the ice cream comparison. The suggestion that someone or something could be up in the sky eating the ice cream makes him think that angels live in the sky, and he revises his poem using that image.

After Graham shares his revised poem, Natalia writes one in which she compares the ocean to the sky on the ground. (See Figure 4.23.)

Figure 4.22 Graham's Poem "Clouds" After the Peer-Editing Lesson, Kindergarten

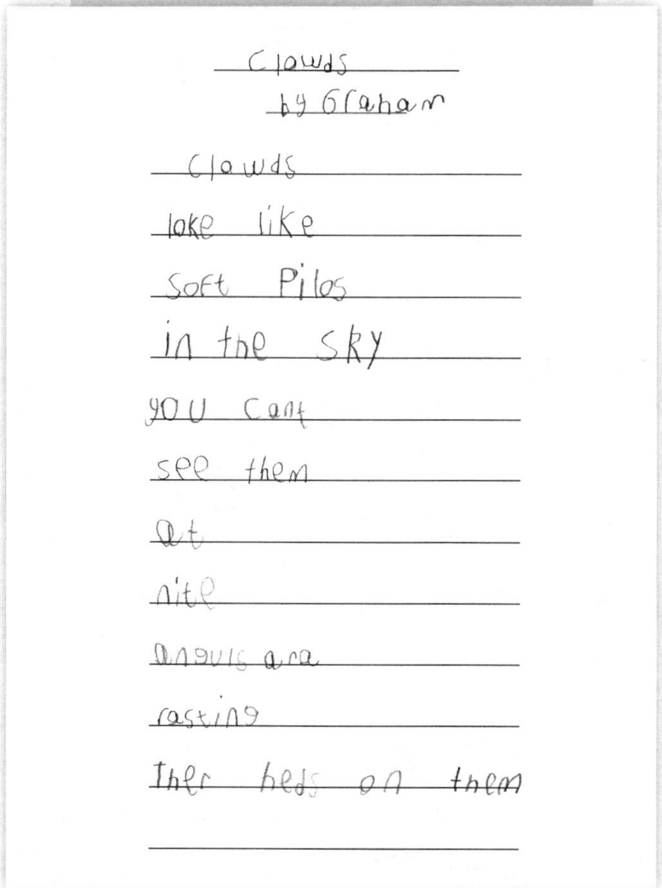

Figure 4.23 Natalia's Poem "Ocean," Kindergarten

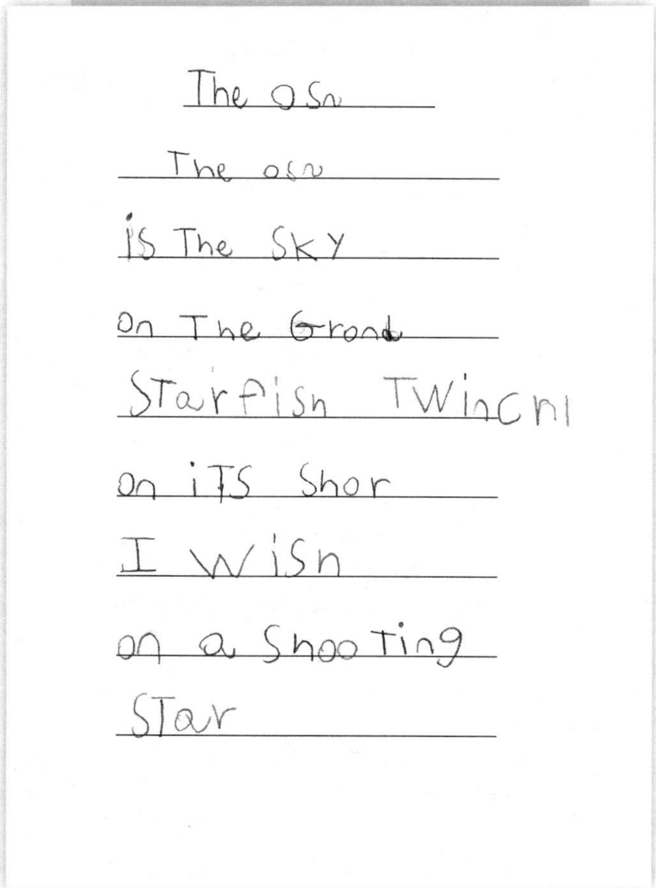

May be photocopied for classroom use. © 2015 by Lisa Eickholdt from *Learning from Classmates: Using Students' Writing as Mentor Texts*. Portsmouth, NH: Heinemann.

Things to keep in mind - - - - - - - - - - - - - -

Immersion

* Expose students to the genre: Immerse students before they write by reading lots of great mentor texts. This activity will give them a sense of the genre.

* Chart it: Work with students to highlight the key features of a genre. Post these on a class anchor chart.

* Choose wisely: Choose mentor texts that are filled with great craft so you can return to these same texts over and over again for different teaching points.

* Give a copy: Provide students with a copy of the mentor text to store in their writing folders. They can then return to the text over and over again as they are writing.

* Name it: Be sure to name the writing technique for students. Remember, naming something makes it repeatable.

* Don't assume compliance: Just because you tell students to do something, don't assume they will. Instead, help students understand why they should use a certain writing technique. Explain why it's effective. Show students how it will help them as writers or how it improves their writing.

Assessment

* Begin at the beginning: Assess your group of students before a unit of study so you can plan lessons that are responsive to their needs.

* Determine what you value: Decide what writing traits you value most. Then, search for these in your students' work.

* Choose a few teaching points: Decide what your students need to learn. Choose several goals for your group and plan lessons that support these goals.

* Search for student mentor texts: As you search for needs, search for possible mentor texts. Though many of your kids need help with a certain writing technique, there will be a few students who don't. Use these students' writing as mentor texts in your lessons.

* Repeat the process: Reassess your group midway through a unit to determine how best to meet students' current needs. Set new goals and create new lessons to support these needs.

* Reflect: Analyze your groups' writing after a study. Their writing is a mirror of your teaching. Reflect on how you can improve as a teacher.

Lessons

* Make a plan: Now that you have student writing that you want to use as a mentor text, plan how best to use the piece. Use the planning guide to help.

* Ensure the text is easy to read: Enlarge the mentor text by using a document camera, rewriting it on a large piece of chart paper, or displaying it through your computer.

* Ensure the text is easy to hear: Consider whether you or the student author will read the text to the group. If the student is reading it aloud, be ready to scaffold him or her as needed. Make sure students can both see and hear the mentor text.

* Choose a teaching method: Consider the best way to teach with the mentor text. Will you use a show-and-tell lesson? A before-and-after lesson? An inquiry or working-backward lesson? What is the best way to teach with this student's text?

* Get them started on the carpet: After you demonstrate in a lesson, get kids started. Consider what type of guided practice will work best. Will kids help you? Will they try it in their own piece? Will they help a classmate? What will be most effective?

* Repeat the process: After your lesson, begin searching for student writing to use as a mentor text again. Search for mentor texts from students who are doing what you taught in the lesson and from students who are doing something totally new. There isn't one writing teacher in your room; there are many! Start taking advantage of this!

Conferences

* Be optimistic: Examine your students' work with an eye toward the positive. Look beyond surface errors, and search for the good. Beautiful content often hides under tough-to-read handwriting.

* Confer with a double lens: As you work with individual students, keep your group in mind. Ask yourself, "What has this child done that he or she can teach the rest?"

* Record it: Write down anecdotal notes as you confer. Keep track of when you confer with each of your students, what you teach them, and how their writing was used as a mentor text.

* Honor all students: Be sure to use writing from each child in your class as a mentor text. Every child has something worthy to offer. Seek it out!

* Be flexible: Be ready to abandon your lesson plans when something better turns up. When a child does something amazing, be ready to shift gears and teach this wonderful new thing to everyone else.

Works Cited

Anderson, Carl. 2009. *Strategic Writing Conferences: Smart Conversations That Move Young Writers Forward.* Portsmouth, NH: Heinemann.

———. 2009. *Carl on Camera: Introducing Strategic Writing Conferences.* Produced by *first*Hand: Heinemann. DVD.

———. 2005. *Assessing Writers.* Portsmouth, NH: Heinemann.

———. 2000. *How's It Going? A Practical Guide to Conferring with Student Writers.* Portsmouth, NH: Heinemann.

Angelillo, Janet. 2003. *Writing About Reading.* Portsmouth, NH: Heinemann.

Atwell, Nancy. 2007. *Lessons That Change Writers.* Portsmouth, NH: *first*Hand.

Bomer, Katherine. 2010. *Hidden Gems: Naming and Teaching from the Brilliance in Every Student's Writing.* Portsmouth, NH: Heinemann.

Caine, Karen. 2008. *Writing to Persuade.* Portsmouth, NH: Heinemann.

Calkins, Lucy. 2013. *Writing Pathways Grades K–5: Performance Assessments and Learning Progressions.* Portsmouth, NH: *first*Hand.

———. 2003. *The Nuts and Bolts of Teaching Writing.* Portsmouth, NH: *first*Hand.

———. 1994. *The Art of Teaching Writing.* Portsmouth, NH: Heinemann.

Calkins, Lucy, and Colleen Gillette. 2006. *Breathing Life into Essays.* Portsmouth, NH: *first*Hand.

Calkins, Lucy and Marjorie Martinelli. 2006. *Launching the Writing Workshop.* Portsmouth, NH: *first*Hand.

Calkins, Lucy, and Abby Oxenhorn. 2003. *Small Moments: Personal Narrative Writing.* Portsmouth, NH: *first*Hand.

Calkins, Lucy, and Laura Pessah. 2003. *Nonfiction Writing: Procedures and Reports.* Portsmouth, NH: *first*Hand.

Cambourne, Brian. 1988. *Natural Learning and the Acquisition of Literacy in the Classroom.* New York: Scholastic.

Culham, Ruth. 2003. *6+1 Traits of Writing: The Complete Guide, Grades 3 and Up.* New York: Scholastic.

Daiker, Donald. 1989. "Learning to Praise." *Writing and Response: Theory, Practice, and Research.* Urbana, IL: National Council of Teachers of English, 103–113.

Dorfman, Lynne, and Rose Capelli. 2007. *Mentor Texts: Teaching Writing Through Children's Literature.* Portland, ME: Stenhouse.

Fletcher, Ralph. 1993. *What a Writer Needs.* Portsmouth, NH: Heinemann.

Graves, Donald. 1995. *A Fresh Look at Writing.* Portsmouth, NH: Heinemann.

———. 1983. *Writing: Teachers and Children at Work.* Portsmouth, NH: Heinemann.

Hartman, Amanda, and Julia Mooney. 2013. *Lessons from Masters: Improving Narrative Writing*. Portsmouth, NH: *first*Hand.

Harvey, Stephanie. 2014. Comprehension, Collaboration, and Inquiry Presentation. 13 July, Denver, CO.

Harvey, Stephanie, and Anne Goudvis. 2007. *Strategies That Work: Teaching Comprehension for Engagement and Understanding*. Portland, ME: Stenhouse.

Heard, Georgia. 1999. *Awakening the Heart: Exploring Poetry in Elementary and Middle School*. Portsmouth, NH: Heinemann.

Johnston, Peter. 2004. *Choice Words: How Our Language Affects Children's Learning*. Portland, ME: Stenhouse.

Knudson, R. 1995. "Writing Experiences, Attitudes, and Achievement of First to Sixth Graders." *Journal of Educational Research* 89: 90–97.

Lane, Barry. 1999. *Reviser's Toolbox*. Shoreham, VT: Discover Writing Press.

Martinelli, Marjorie, and Kristine Mraz. 2012. *Smarter Charts K–2: Optimizing an Instructional Staple to Create Independent Readers and Writers*. Portsmouth, NH: Heinemann.

Murray, Donald. 2009. *The Essential Don Murray: Lessons from America's Greatest Writing Teacher*. Portsmouth, NH: Heinemann.

National Governors Association Center for Best Practices (NGA Center) and Council of Chief State School Officers (CCSSO). 2011. *Common Core State Standards for English Language Arts and Literacy*. Washington, DC: NGA Center and CCSSO.

Pearson, P. David, and Margaret Gallagher. 1983. "The Instruction of Reading Comprehension." *Contemporary Educational Psychology* 8: 317–44.

Portalupi, JoAnn, and Ralph Fletcher. 2004. *Teaching the Qualities of Writing*. Portsmouth, NH: *first*Hand.

———. 2001. *Writing Workshop: The Essential Guide*. Portsmouth, NH: Heinemann.

———. 1998. *Craft Lessons: Teaching Writing K–8*. Portland, MN: Stenhouse.

Ray, Katie. 2006. *Study Driven: A Framework for Planning Units of Study in the Writing Workshop*. Portsmouth, NH: Heinemann.

———. 1999. *Wondrous Words: Writers and Writing in the Elementary Classroom*. Urbana, IL: National Council of Teachers of English.

Rhodes, Lynne, and Nancy Shanklin. 1993. *Windows into Literacy: Assessing Learners K–8*. Portsmouth, NH: Heinemann.

Rist, Ronald. 2000. "The Enduring Dilemmas of Class and Color in America." *Harvard Educational Review* 70 (3): 257–301.

Schunk, Dale, and Antoinette Hanson. 1985. "Peer Models: Influence on Children's Self-Efficacy and Achievement." *Journal of Educational Psychology* 77: 313–22.

Smith, Frank. 1998. *The Book of Learning and Forgetting.* New York: Teachers College Press.

———. 1994. *Understanding Reading. A Psycholinguistic Analysis of Reading and Learning to Read.* Hillsdale, NJ: Erlbaum Associates.

Spandel, Vickie. 2001. *Creating Writers Through 6-Trait Writing Assessment and Instruction.* New York: Allyn & Bacon.

Taylor, Sarah and Lucy Calkins. 2008. *A Quick Guide to Teaching Persuasive Writing, K–2.* Portsmouth, NH: *first*Hand.

Vygotsky, Lev. 1978. *Mind in Society: The Development of Higher Psychological Processes.* Edited and translated by M. Cole, V. Alfred-Steiner, S. Scribner, and E. Souberman. Cambridge, MA: Harvard University Press.